KEEP
YOUR
LOVE
ON

365
DAILY DEVOTIONS
FOR COUPLES

BroadStreet
PUBLISHING

Keep Your Love On helped me finally understand how to build and protect healthy relationships. Danny's teaching on connection, communication, and boundaries made everything so clear and easy to understand. Learning and living the KYLO message daily has changed my life and relationships forever!

—**Christian Zamora**, husband and father

KYLO was a Holy Spirit-led choice for me, and it has changed my life in many ways. Not only has my marriage been restored, but other relationships are also more intimate with proper boundaries that keep me empowered, whole, and healthy. I am able to keep connections strong while also knowing how to say "no" to things I feel uncomfortable with.

—**Jordan Davis**, youth pastor and business owner

I grew up in a family with a dysfunctional communication style (one parent passive, one aggressive, and everything swept under the rug with appearances being the most important thing). Sadly, I saw this continue into my own family after marriage. Once I was introduced to KYLO, everything improved in our family: my connection with my husband, my connections with my children (especially how I parented), and connections with others. We have been able to break the cycle! Hallelujah! This has recently become evident as my parents after forty years of marriage are struggling in their relationship and communication. Of course, I just referred them to *Keep Your Love On*, and they ordered it. Now I have hope!

—**Emily Johnson**, wife and mother

I have spent years looking for help for my family and our relationships. The principles of KYLO brought tremendous hope and healing into our lives. I told my family "I am not good at this, but I am determined to become good at it." Now as my own life has changed, I am seeing my family become whole and healthy.

—**Don Trail**, husband, father, and businessman

Last year, our ministry went through a difficult season where relationships with a few of our young leaders fractured and blew apart. We are so thankful that The Life Academy and KYLO principles were made known to us. We immediately began a heart internship with our leaders and missionaries using these teachings. Four months in, we are blown away! We are seeing so much growth and can honestly say we are the healthiest community we have ever been. By cultivating an environment of powerful people who are choosing love over fear with a desire for connection, operating in respectful communication and healthy boundaries, we are changing the world! We are forever grateful to Danny and his KYLO Team.

—**Cheryl Smith**, co-founder and pastor of
Eastgate House of Prayer Mission Base

About ten years ago, our family was in crisis. My wife had a breakdown, and I was at a loss for how to stay connected to God, to her, and to myself in this time. KYLO gave me the tools I needed to be a husband and father who was both empathetic and empowering. As a result, we remained connected and hopeful through this season. KYLO has literally changed my life, I can't recommend it enough.

—**Dave Hill**, director of Bethel Kids, founder of
HeartSmart TV, husband, and father

I feel like my wife Angie and I have always had a great marriage, but the KYLO principles have helped us take it to a deeper level. Before KYLO, I never realized how much I was choosing to love her at a safe distance because of fear, rather than pursuing the goal of connection. KYLO has given us the courage to walk the journey of setting aside our old habits and fears in order to make intimacy our target.

—**Josh Haas**, pastor

Keeping your love on meant learning how to love myself, set healthy boundaries, and manage "me" no matter what was happening around me. Every area of my life—my family connections, professional relationships, business and ministry—continues to be strengthened beyond what I could imagine as I practice inserting love where fear used to be. Living in love feels like freedom.

—**Bernii Godwin**, wife, stepmom, school social worker

The tools KYLO provided me in my life have changed the legacy of my family. Choosing love over fear means I can approach conflict to understand others, rather than force agreement. Not only that, but I now have the confidence to participate and set boundaries for respectful communication for myself and others in any situation.

—**Jayden Godwin**, husband, father, and founder of Rise Up Catering

The *Keep Your Love On* message changed not only my life but my marriage. Understanding that I have the ability to get my needs met and that God is the supplier of all my needs took the pressure off my husband and allowed us both to rely upon God, seeing each other as a way God can supply our needs not the only way. It was a game changer to realize God was not limited by our capacity; He is infinitely creative and able to meet all of our needs according to His riches and glory. This opened my husband and I up to partnering together to find solutions.

—**Genesis Eakes**, president and founder of Genesis Eakes International Corporation

Keep Your Love On has given me the tools to make love believable. Jesus said, "No greater love has any man that they would lay down their life for another" and KYLO teaches the practical tools to make that an active expression. My life has been so impacted, as well as the culture in my marriage, in our home, and even in our church. I'm forever grateful to have learned these powerful tools and principles.

—**Katieann Browning**, senior leader of Resolute Ministries

BroadStreet Publishing® Group, LLC.
Savage, Minnesota, USA
Broadstreetpublishing.com

KEEP YOUR LOVE ON: 365 Daily Devotions
© 2022 by Danny Silk

978-1-4245-6394-4
978-1-4245-6395-1 (eBook)

Design by Chris Garborg | garborgdesign.com
Compiled and edited by Michelle Winger | literallyprecise.com

Printed in China.

22   23   24   25   26   27   7   6   5   4   3   2   1

"My command is this:
Love each other
as I have loved you."

John 15:12 NIV

INTRODUCTION

Relationships are vital to becoming a whole person. I wrote *Keep Your Love On* to help people build, strengthen, and heal their relational connections. This has been my personal mission statement for the last twenty years.

As a husband, father, foster parent, group home staff member, social worker, program director, group facilitator, pastor, author, speaker, or leader, my goal has remained the same—I am alive to help people connect and stay connected.

Keep Your Love On (KYLO) is a mindset. It is a heart condition. It's something no one can make you do, and no one can keep you from doing. It is a force with a life of its own. Once this force begins to build momentum in your life, you will be able to love fully and do just about anything in life. Keeping your love on creates fearlessness and deep vulnerability.

The goal of life-long love is something everyone desires. It is the hope of every young couple who gaze into each other's eyes and believe that this is "The One." It is the commitment young parents make when they look into the innocent face of their first child. However, quality love relationships do not happen by accident. Real love is built the old-fashioned way—through hard work. And if you learn to manage the very best of who you are, the all-elusive intimacy experience you crave will be well within your grasp.

This devotional includes quick daily readings, thought-provoking questions, and Scriptures that help reinforce the three basic principles of the KYLO book—connecting, communicating, and setting boundaries.

I pray that you will continue to find hope and healing on your journey. I am grateful that you are among those who are learning how to love well.

Peace,

Danny

I CHOOSE YOU

> "You did not choose me, but I chose you and appointed you
> so that you might go and bear fruit."
>
> JOHN 15:16 NIV

When you said your vows at your wedding ceremony, you may not have understood the significance of what you were saying. You probably had no idea what you were signing up for. At the time, the choice may have seemed easy or even fun, but when your journey carries you into difficult situations, choosing your spouse can become the test of a lifetime.

You have chosen to be committed to someone for life. You will be challenged and invited to hold to that choice again and again. Today, as you focus on your relationship with your spouse, speak these words of devotion to each other: "I choose you."

Jesus, please help us to choose each other each day through all the challenges and tests. We want to bear good fruit as we choose love in our relationship.

How can you make the foundation of your relationship with your spouse an "I choose you" relationship?

VERBAL REMINDER

I will not be negligent to remind you always of these things,
though you know and are established in the present truth.

2 PETER 1:12 NKJV

It is good to remind yourself of the choice you made on your
wedding day. When you confirm your desire to stick with that
choice, you help ease anxiety and establish instead the comfort,
affection, and security necessary to remain connected. You
show your spouse that you are continuing to choose them even
when things are rough.

It is normal to wrestle with the commitment to that choice.
You won't always get it right, but a constant verbal reminder
will help you hold fast to each other and keep you accountable
before one another and before God. It ultimately teaches you
how to keep your love on.

*Heavenly Father, we choose to be accountable to You with our
choices. We want to lessen the anxiety in our relationship and be
a source of comfort and affection for each other. Help us to stay
committed to our choice of love.*

What can you do to remind your spouse of your choice today?

HIS CHOICE

God showed his great love for us by sending Christ
to die for us while we were still sinners.

ROMANS 5:8 NLT

The foundation of true, lasting relationships is the commitment to choose love. This is how God has drawn you into relationship with Himself. He chose you in the most difficult of circumstances—while you were still in sin, when you were His enemy.

God's side of the relationship does not depend upon your choice, but entirely upon His. You have to learn how to build your relationship with Him and others upon the foundation of your choice. You can't just love each other when it is easy. You choose to love through the challenges.

God, thank You for showing us the depth of Your love when You sent Your Son to die for us. You chose to love us when we were still sinners. Help us to love each other even when we are struggling in our relationship.

*How can you build your relationship with God
and with your spouse on the foundation of your choice?*

BACKWARDS

Be devoted to one another in love.
Honor one another above yourselves.
ROMANS 12:10 NIV

You are headed for trouble if you try to build your relationship on a "you chose me" basis. It is natural instinct to like people who like you and to choose people who choose you. But if all your relationships are based solely on your natural impulse to return liking for liking, you will have problems. What happens when you no longer like someone?

Liking is conditional, and it changes. If the condition for your relationship is "You chose me" instead of "I choose you," the relationship is doomed to change and will probably collapse as soon as the liking goes away. Make it your mission to continue to choose each other, so that when liking is lacking, your relationship remains intact.

Jesus, Your devotion to us is unmatched. Help us continue to choose each other and honor each other even when we are finding it difficult to like each other. Show us how to draw from Your example of devoted love.

How can you turn your relationship from "you chose me" to "I choose you" today?

TAKE RESPONSIBILITY

> [Love] always protects, always trusts,
> always hopes, always perseveres.
> 1 CORINTHIANS 13:7 NIV

A healthy, lasting relationship is built between two people who choose each other and take full responsibility for that choice. At the altar, you took responsibility for your part in the relationship. You committed to loving your spouse for better or worse, richer or poorer, in sickness and health, to love and to cherish, as long as you live. You didn't stand and proclaim what your spouse would do for you.

Your choice for each other is based on who you are, what you want, and what you are committed to doing. Take responsibility today to love, to serve, to protect, and to be faithful to each other no matter what.

God, always seems like an impossible word. Only Your love can always protect, trust, hope, and persevere. Help us to focus on ourselves and not on our spouses as we take individual responsibility for loving like You love.

What does taking responsibility in your choice to love your spouse look like to you?

BECOMING POWERFUL

We are each responsible
for our own conduct.
GALATIANS 6:5 NLT

In order to be able to make and keep commitments to enduring, intimate relationships, you need to be powerful. Powerful people take responsibility for their lives. Were you taught how to be responsible for your choices? A lot of people weren't. They don't know that they can be powerful, or even that they should be.

To build healthy relationships with your spouse and others, you have to become powerful. You need to choose who you want to be with, what you are going to pursue in life, and how you are going to go after it. And you need to take responsibility for each of those decisions when they are made.

God, show us what it means to be powerful in our relationship with each other. We need You to give us wisdom and strength to make decisions that are honoring to You and to our relationship.

How can you become more powerful in your relationships?

LANGUAGE SHIFT

I can do everything through Christ,
who gives me strength.
PHILIPPIANS 4:13 NLT

I can't. I have to. When you use these phrases, it reveals a powerless mindset. It is as if you are saying the decision is being made by someone other than you, and you have no choice in the matter. You are reluctant to take responsibility for the decision, so it feels better to say that someone or something else is making you act.

If you are powerless, you might also catch yourself saying, "I'll try…" just in case you don't come through on a commitment or promise. Change your language that is rooted in powerlessness and believe that you have the power to manage yourself.

Jesus, You have given us the strength to do everything You ask of us. You can help us change our powerless mindset into a powerful one and give us the ability to manage ourselves. Help our language to be full of confidence and ability.

What powerless language do you find yourself using?
What can you do to shift it?

STAND AGAINST FEAR

I prayed to the LORD, and he answered me.
He freed me from all my fears.
PSALM 34:4 NLT

When you are powerless, you believe that most things and
people in the world are more powerful than you are, and that
is scary. Anxiety becomes your defining, driving force, and
you feel as if life is out of your control. Powerless people have
a deep need to suppress their abiding fear—fear of loss, pain,
death, abandonment, and more.

If you think you don't have the power to deal with your fear,
then your only hope is to persuade other people to do it for
you. You rely on them sharing their power with you because
you feel like you don't have any of your own. When you take a
stand against fear, you stop trying to manipulate and control
others, and you take responsibility for making yourself feel safe
and happy.

*Jesus, we are not powerless people. You have freed us from all
our fears, and You are in control of every situation life brings.
We say today that we will not be afraid. We resist the urge to
manipulate and control others. In You, we will find our safety
and our happiness.*

What fears do you need to take a stand against today?

NOT A CONSUMER

"Whatever you ask in prayer, believing,
you will receive it all."
MATTHEW 21:22 NASB

Have you ever wanted to be with someone just because
you want some of their happiness to rub off on you? It's not
uncommon to want this; however, you have to be careful that
you don't become consumers, sucking the happiness out of
people until they are left dry.

The same can be said for resources of love, joy, and comfort.
If you don't have those yourself, you tend to look for them
in others. But you will never be satisfied unless you get what
you need from God. He can give you your own supply of the
resources you see and desire in others. All you have to do is ask!

*God, we know the only place to find true happiness is in You.
Help us to be satisfied by Your love, joy, and peace. Thank You
for those around us who have an abundance of these resources.
Teach us to learn from them instead of trying to take from them.*

*How have you been approaching your relationship
as a consumer? What can you do to change that?*

BLAME GAME

If we confess our sins, he is faithful and just and will forgive us our sins and purify us from all unrighteousness.

1 JOHN 1:9 NIV

It is hard to admit when you are wrong. Most people don't like to take responsibility for their poor choices or the consequences that came out of making them. Powerless people often blame the messes they make on other people. The reason their life, marriage, child, finances, job, or whatever is the way it is has nothing to do with their choices. In their minds, someone else created the life they're living.

You have the power to create your own life. It starts with taking responsibility for your choices. When you fail, ask God and others for forgiveness, admitting you were wrong and moving forward in grace.

God, please forgive us for the messes we have made in our relationship. Thank You for being faithful to forgive us and cleanse us. Help us to make good choices and move forward in grace and forgiveness.

Do you need to ask for forgiveness for a poor choice?
Do that today and press on!

CONTROLLED SPACE

The LORD is my strength and my shield;
in him my heart trusts, and I am helped;
my heart exults,
and with my song I give thanks to him.
PSALM 28:7 ESV

If you live in an anxiety-driven environment, take a close look at who is controlling your space. Powerless people create a thin veneer of safety and calm that covers underlying currents of control and intimidation. Those who enter their atmosphere quickly learn to shape up and go with the program—until it dawns on them that they will never be safe to be themselves.

When you are confronted with this realization, you have a couple different options. You can stay in the anxiety and submit to the control of the powerless people, or you can move. Sometimes you choose to stay because it feels safe, but the same protection that shields you from "scary" people prevents you from developing intimate connections with safe people. You can trust God to show you the way to peace. It might require stepping out of what feels comfortable, but it will be worth it.

Lord Jesus, we trust You to take care of us and show us the path to peace. We want to follow You out of anxiety and into a safe environment where we can both thrive.

Does fear of relationship keep you stuck in an anxiety-driven environment? How can you create a different atmosphere?

ROLE PLAY

Trust in the LORD and do good.
Then you will live safely in the land and prosper.
PSALM 37:3 NLT

The classic relational dynamic created by powerless people is called triangulation. When you believe that other people are scary, unsafe, and more powerful than you are, and when you think you need to get them to meet your needs, then you have three possible roles to play in a relationship: the victim, the bad guy, or the rescuer.

If you're the victim, you look for a rescuer to make you feel safe and happy. If you're the bad guy, you use control and intimidation to protect yourself or get someone to meet your needs. If you're a rescuer, you take responsibility for someone else's life in an attempt to feel powerful. None of these are the roles you are destined for. God has so much better for you. He is your strength and your provider. Go to Him with your needs.

God, help us not to play roles we are not supposed to play. We want to be powerful. We trust You with our needs and believe that You want the best for us as individuals and for our relationship.

Can you see yourself operating in any of these roles? How can you change?

FIRSTBORN RESCUER

Encourage one another and build each other up,
just as in fact you are doing.

1 THESSALONIANS 5:11 NIV

If you or your spouse is a firstborn child (in any sense), you may be a prime candidate for the rescuer role. Firstborns are often trained from the time they are little to take care of people who are less powerful. You may have been asked to pick up after younger siblings, watch them at the park, or help keep them out of trouble.

Rescuing people from themselves and taking responsibility for their lives is a familiar role, and it feels like love. But it actually can create unhealthy codependence. You need to develop the ability to say no to taking on others' responsibilities, so you don't end up exerting your power over others. You can empower them to become powerful people themselves when you encourage them to take the responsibility that is rightfully theirs.

Jesus, help us to encourage everyone around us to become powerful. We don't want to take on responsibilities that don't belong to us. Teach us how to say no to unhealthy habits.

Do you see yourself as being prone to rescuing? How can you turn this around and empower people instead?

NEED TO CONTROL

You will keep in perfect peace
those whose minds are steadfast,
because they trust in you.
ISAIAH 26:3 NIV

Do either of you feel like you live in a perpetual state of anxiety? This can lead to you feeling like you always need to be in control. When you add someone to your life, you become increasingly anxious because now you feel the need to control that person as well. You may feel threatened if your spouse makes their own decisions.

When you become a powerful person, you allow both parties in a relationship to make their own decisions and take responsibility for them. Your marriage will benefit greatly from this. You will begin to feel safe in the relationship and come to understand that your spouse's love for you is freely offered, not coerced in any way.

God, it is difficult not to want to control each other. Help us to understand the importance of letting each person take responsibility for themselves. We want to have a healthy marriage where we both feel safe and where anxiety cannot dwell.

How does the need for control hinder a relationship?

POWER PLAY

Turn away from evil and do good.
Search for peace, and work to maintain it.
PSALM 34:14 NLT

If your relational bond is built on mutual control, it simply cannot produce anything remotely like safety, love, or trust. It can only produce more fear, pain, distrust, punishment, and misery. While you may hope your relationship will be defined by happiness and security, the reality is when you and your spouse try to exercise control over each other, you both just become miserable.

You might find yourselves using various tactics, such as getting upset, withdrawing, nagging, ridiculing, pouting, crying, or getting angry to pressure, manipulate, and punish one another into keeping the power play going. Anxiety escalates and neither of you actually ends up feeling powerful at all. To create an environment of love and safety that isn't tenuous or fleeting, you both must recognize your need for control and submit it to God.

Father, help us to search for peace and to put in the work required to maintain it. We want love to be the driving force in our marriage. Help us to let go of our control and hand the reins to You.

Do you feel like you are engaged in a power play with each other? How can you create an atmosphere of security?

SET THE STANDARD

A servant of the Lord must not quarrel but must be kind to everyone, be able to teach, and be patient with difficult people. Gently instruct those who oppose the truth. Perhaps God will change those people's hearts, and they will learn the truth.

2 TIMOTHY 2:24-25 NLT

When you think of someone as being powerful, do you imagine they are loud, overbearing, or commanding? Would it surprise you to know that a controlling, dominating person is the very opposite of a powerful person? Powerful people do not try to control other people. They know it doesn't work, and that it's not their job. They understand that their job is to control themselves.

Operating in a powerful manner means you can consciously and deliberately create the environment in which you want to live. You don't try to get people to respect you; you create a respectful environment by showing respect. You deliberately set the standard for how you expect to be treated by the way you treat others. When you consistently act in responsible, respectful, and loving ways, it becomes clear that the only people who can get close to you are those who know how to show respect, be responsible, and love well.

Jesus, help us to be respectful in the way we treat each other. We want to set a standard of honor and respect in our home.

How can you begin to create an environment of respect in your home?

ON FULL BLAST

Be supernaturally infused with strength through your life-union with the Lord Jesus. Stand victorious with the force of his explosive power flowing in and through you.

EPHESIANS 6:10 TPT

Life does not happen to powerful people. Powerful people are happening—they are happening all the time. They are like a hose that is on full blast in the middle of a mud puddle. The mud does not go up into the hose and contaminate it. Powerful people are not affected or infected by their environment. They refuse to be victims of others, and they do not try to control other people.

In a good marriage relationship, both individuals are powerful people. They don't need to control each other, and they don't play the victim or allow themselves to become the victim. Learn how to be hoses on full blast that operate in sync instead of fighting against each other. Wash the mud of bad habits away!

Jesus, You give us supernatural strength to stand victoriously and take life by the horns. We choose today not to be victims who are affected and controlled by our environment. Help us to stand and fight for our relationship together.

What can you do to help each other become hoses on full blast?

No Other Options

Every child of God overcomes the world, for our faith is the victorious power that triumphs over the world. So who are the world conquerors, defeating its power? Those who believe that Jesus is the Son of God.

1 John 5:4-5 TPT

Powerful people require others to be powerful around them. When you encounter a powerless person, don't be tempted to dive into their problem. Listen to their sob story and ask, "What are you going to do about that? What have you tried? What else could you try?" These questions confront powerless people with their responsibility and their capacity to make choices and control themselves.

The only options you want to offer powerless people is to become powerful, make choices, and control themselves. When someone fails to get you to offer any additional help, they will either change and begin living powerfully, or they will find someone else to dump on. Be strong and encourage others to do the same!

Father, thank You for giving us the power to overcome the ways of the world and to control ourselves. Help us to ask the right questions in the right moments. We want to make our own choices and take responsibility for them.

Is there someone in your relational sphere who needs you to encourage them to live powerfully?

EMBRACE THE DAY

This is the day the LORD has made.
We will rejoice and be glad in it.

PSALM 118:24 NLT

You can choose the kind of day you will have. There is nothing saying that you have to relegate yourself to reacting to whatever goes on around you. You can take responsibility for your decisions and the consequences of those decisions—even your mistakes and failures. You can respond to today and create your tomorrows.

Don't just hope for a good day. Don't hope people will be nice to you. Don't hope for respect. Choose it all. You will have a good day because you are a powerful person. You have a vision for your life, and you can use the situations of the day, whether positive or negative, to direct yourself toward that vision.

Jesus, thank You for today. Thank You for another opportunity to choose to have a good day. We are so grateful for life and for love. Thank You for the grace to learn from our mistakes and choose differently next time. You are so good, and because of that alone, we can rejoice in this day.

How can you and your spouse encourage each other to embrace each day with faith?

YES AND NO

"Just say a simple, 'Yes, I will,' or 'No, I won't.'
Anything beyond this is from the evil one."
MATTHEW 5:37 NLT

Popular opinion or the pressure of others does not need to sway your language or decisions. To operate in a position of power, know what you want and communicate your desires. Say, "I will. I do. I am." Use yes and no answers and stick to them. When others try to manipulate, charm, or threaten you, be firm. Don't change your mind.

A powerful person's choice to love will stand, no matter what others do or say. When powerful people say, "I love you," there's nothing that can stop them. Their love is not dependent on being loved in return. It is dependent on their powerful ability to say yes and carry out that decision. Become powerful in order to protect your love from external forces including other people.

God, it can be very difficult to stick with our commitments when pressures abound. Thank You for giving us strength to carry out what we have said we will do. Help us to protect our relationship from destructive forces. We choose to continue in love.

What can you do to say yes to loving your spouse today?

WHO YOU ARE

O LORD, you have searched me
and known me.
PSALM 139:1 ESV

Can you be who you say you are on a consistent basis? When
you know how to be yourself and are comfortable with it,
you invite those around you to be themselves as well. Only
powerful people can create a safe place to know and be known
intimately. They say, "I can be me around you and you can be
you around me."

You and your spouse don't need to control each other, nor
should you want to. You can have a mutual agreement of
respect and honor in which you both work to protect your
connection. You stay tied together by the strength of the love
you have built, not by the illusion that you can control each
other or that either of you need a rescuer.

*Creator God, thank You that You know each of us so intimately.
Help us to be authentic before You and with each other. We want
to honor and respect each other, living in a way that protects
and builds our connection.*

How can you invite each other to be yourselves?

TRUTH REVEALED

Guide me in your truth and teach me,
for you are God my Savior,
and my hope is in you all day long.

PSALM 25:5 NIV

Sometimes people experience difficult situations that can start a cycle of victimization. If you continue to recreate this victimized reality, it will stop you from pursuing being powerful. No matter where you go or what happens to you, you will identify yourself as a victim. You can repent from falling into this lifestyle that creates powerlessness.

Repenting means changing the way you think. First, you need to identify the lies you believe and the influence those lies have in your life. Once you identify the lies, renounce them, and break your agreement with them. Then ask the Holy Spirit to reveal the truth.

In the name of Jesus, we renounce these lies. We nail them to the cross of Jesus Christ and send it away from us, never to return again. Holy Spirit, what truth would You like to give us in place of those lies? Show us today.

Rebuke the lies you have believed and ask the Holy Spirit to give you truth in their place. Write down the words of truth that He speaks to you.

MOST POWERFUL CHOICE

We love, because He first loved us.

1 JOHN 4:19 NASB

Often lies become deeply rooted in a person's core, requiring consistent work to dig them out and replace them with the truth. If you grew up in an abusive, powerless environment, you might need someone who can help you identify and renounce those lies. No matter what, know that every step on the journey to getting free and being a powerful person is worth it. Choosing to say yes to a life of responsibility and wholeness will be one filled with adventure and joy.

Do not let powerlessness and a victim mentality steal from you any longer. You are a powerful person who can make powerful decisions. And more importantly, you are a powerful person who can choose to love because God chose to love you. Choosing to love is the most powerful choice you could ever make and is more rewarding than you could ever imagine.

God, thank You for choosing to love us. We can only love You and each other because You showed us what it means to love. Help us to see the lies that have held us back and show us the truth instead.

How can you choose the most powerful choice today?

ESSENTIAL UNDERSTANDING

If it is true that I have gone astray,
my error remains my concern alone.
JOB 19:4 NIV

One of the essentials to having a healthy relationship is understanding that you both can be powerful, responsible people. As long as you both engage that, you will have much more success at creating one of the basic functions of a relationship: to connect with each other.

When one or both of you step away from being powerful, you give yourself permission to be irresponsible. You begin to shift responsibility to somebody else. But when you *choose* to love each other, each person manages their own side of the relationship, and that forms the bond. Don't let powerlessness create a dynamic that undermines your relationship. Choose to remain powerful together.

God, help us to choose love for each other and be responsible for ourselves. We want to be powerful together in You. Thank You that You want us to be successful in connecting with each other and in building our relationship.

What do you do to manage your own side of the relationship?

CHANGE TO THRIVE

Don't copy the behavior and customs of this world, but let God transform you into a new person by changing the way you think. Then you will learn to know God's will for you which is good and pleasing and perfect.

ROMANS 12:2 NLT

When a couple is comprised of two powerful people, the relationship can thrive. If both are powerless, the connection between the two is undermined, and the anxiety dynamic increases tremendously because neither person feels responsible for anything that is happening. The focus in these relationships then becomes about managing each other instead of taking personal responsibility. The goal is, *How can I get you to do what I want so I can be happy?*

In these relationships, where two people are trying to control each other, and neither one is working on controlling themselves, the connection is damaged. If you see yourself in this situation, take heart! Change is possible. Begin to take responsibility for yourself and encourage your spouse to do the same. Become powerful together so your relationship can thrive.

God, we need You to transform the way we think. We want to walk in Your will and not in the ways of the world. Help us to manage ourselves and take responsibility for our actions. May we be pleasing to You in the way we live.

How can you create a thriving relationship with your spouse?

EQUAL RESPONSIBILITY

The one who plants and the one who waters are equally important and on the same team, but each will be rewarded for his own work.

1 CORINTHIANS 3:8 TPT

If your relationship consists of one powerful person and one powerless person, the powerful person may believe they are responsible both for what they can bring to the relationship and also for what the other person contributes. A dependent or codependent relationship is formed when both parties believe that one person is responsible for both people's happiness, misery, and everything in between. The powerful person will often take the blame for the other's irresponsibility, and they may try really hard to make that person happy, which is impossible.

It is not either spouse's job to control the other's happiness, anger, or anything else. You both have to stop feeding a dynamic where one person feels like they are the only one responsible for the relationship. Either begin to take responsibility for yourself and become powerful, or refuse to take responsibility for the powerless one, and encourage them toward becoming powerful themselves.

Thank You, Jesus, that You have created us with different gifts and abilities. Help us to understand that we are on the same team, and we are equally responsible for the success of the team.

Do both spouses feel a right amount of responsibility for the relationship?

THE RIGHTFUL HALF

"I, the LORD search the heart
and examine the mind,
to reward each person according to their conduct,
according to what their deeds deserve."

JEREMIAH 17:10 NIV

The healthiest marriages have two powerful people choosing to be in a committed relationship with each other. Both individuals have decided they will manage themselves and they will respect their spouse's choice to manage themselves.

Each person agrees to move toward the other person, to choose that person no matter what the circumstance is. But they also require each other to manage their rightful half of the relationship. It is your job to take responsibility for yourself in your relationships. This is true not only with your spouse, but with your family, friends, co-workers, and community members.

God, You say in Your Word that You will reward each of us according to our own behavior. Help us to be mindful of this in our relationship with each other. We want to do what is right by You and create an atmosphere of safety and love in our home.

*In which relationships do you struggle to
take responsibility only for yourself?*

I CAN AND I WILL

He gives power to the weak
and strength to the powerless.

ISAIAH 40:29 NLT

Will you choose to love your spouse for the rest of your life? *I'll try.* If your language often consists of "I'll try" or "I have to" or "I can't," you may need to take some lessons in becoming powerful. If you feel like you have to do something, it means the choice is not yours; something or someone is in charge of you besides yourself. You may experience a lot of anxiety because you feel that something external is more powerful than you.

You might look for control in a relationship, for somebody to rescue you, or for somebody to take the blame for your lack. You may have said, "You're the reason I'm in this shape, why I feel this way, why I don't trust." Someone else is always the reason. Remember, you need to take responsibility for your part in the relationship. Don't allow yourself to be a victim. You can become more powerful than those external forces. Begin using language that says, "I will, I can, I choose to."

Father God, we chose each other on our wedding day, and we choose each other again today. Help us both to be powerful in our relationship. We can and will remain committed to each other because Your grace is sufficient.

What do you need to choose for yourself today?

No Bad Guys

I pray that from his glorious, unlimited resources he will
empower you will inner strength through his Spirit.

EPHESIANS 3:16 NLT

Victims have a unique worldview. They identify themselves as
being powerless and choose to give their power to "bad guys"
they blame for their problems (parents, spouses, bosses, etc.).
This creates a cycle of irresponsibility. Because they have set
their power on someone else, they now have to find a rescuer.
A rescuer swoops in and brings the victim justice. They show
the victim their "love" by taking on the victim's relational
conflict, at the same time removing the victim from the
opportunity and challenge of making responsible choices.

If you find yourself responding like a victim, you need to
remember that there are no bad guys. There are people you
have conflict and disagreements with, and there are people
who make poor choices. If you realize you are in a relationship
with a bad person, and you begin to take responsibility for your
part in the relationship, you exercise your own power. If, after
realizing you are being victimized, you perpetuate the cycle,
you become a volunteer. Choose to get out of the cycle. When
you learn to communicate what you want and stop blaming
others for the condition of your life, you become powerful.

*God, You did not create us to be victims. Help us not to blame
others. Give us strength to become powerful and responsible.*

Can you see how a victim mentality hinders relationships?

HOLD FIRMLY

Remember to stay alert and hold firmly to all that you believe.
Be mighty and full of courage.

1 CORINTHIANS 16:13 TPT

Use powerful language today. Say you will and you can.
Commit to something and do it. Choose your spouse. Do
things you don't feel like doing but are according to the
agreement of taking care of your marriage relationship. Don't
say you have to. Say you choose to. There is no external force
making you do your life. You make the choices that take care of
your relationship. You clean up your part of the mess. You can
and you will.

Learn how to avoid assuming the position of a victim. Require
other people's respect in your relationships. What you think,
feel, and need should be respected. Create processes that
ensure those needs are met and don't live in an ongoing
abusive or irresponsible relationship. Understand that you can
choose to break the abusive cycle by no longer participating in
it or with it. You can do it!

*Jesus, thank You for the power that is available in You. In Your
name, we can live in freedom from abuse and powerlessness.
You have promised to provide everything we need, and we trust
You to do that. Give us powerful words in exchange for weak
words. In You, we are strong.*

*What powerful language can you use today
to ensure you are being respected?*

PUT ON LOVE

In addition to all these things put on love,
which is the perfect bond of unity.
COLOSSIANS 3:14 NASB

When you are in a healthy relationship, both people operate from a knowledge of what they are and aren't responsible for. You tell your spouse what you are doing and don't assume you know what they will do. You each manage yourselves, listen to good information, and set limits. You know that gaining control over the other person is not a thing. Your greatest hope for controlling someone is in controlling yourself. You can only tell yourself what to do.

You have to fight for the power of choice, and you have to continue to choose when things are tough. When you feel disconnected, remind yourself of your choice. You chose to marry your spouse. It might be a scary choice. They could hurt you. But still, you choose them. You keep your love on, and you move toward them, so you can reconnect.

Jesus, sometimes it is hard to choose love. We want to control in an effort to protect ourselves from being hurt. We know You want us to live in unity, bonded by our love for You and for each other. Help us to take the scary step and choose each other today.

How can you choose your spouse again today?

SAFE CONNECTION

"I pray that they will all be one, just as you and I are one—
as you are in me, Father, and I am in you. And may they be
in us so that the world will believe you sent me."

JOHN 17:21 NLT

What is the goal in your marriage relationship? Are you
aware of it? Have you talked about it? The truth is that every
relationship has one of two goals: connection or disconnection.
These goals are revealed by the skill sets people adopt to
achieve them.

If you feel distant in your relationship, you may have developed
the skill of being disconnected through learning how to create
a safe distance from each other. Each moment of each day,
you measure how much distance you need to feel safe around
each other. Sometimes the necessary distance is small, and
other times it's great. You want to shift your goal to one of safe
connection, not safe distance.

*God, we want the goal of our relationship to be connection.
Show us where we have learned to distance ourselves and help
us move back toward each other. We want to be one as You and
the Father are one.*

*What is the goal of your marriage relationship,
and what are you doing to achieve it?*

SOW GENEROUSLY

*The one who sows sparingly will also reap sparingly,
and the one who sows generously will also reap generously.*

2 CORINTHIANS 9:6 NASB

You and your spouse are equally responsible for taking ownership of the goal for your relationship. If you are feeling disconnected, consider how you got yourselves there. Most likely, one or both of you shifted responsibility for the quality of your connection onto your spouse. You put little effort into achieving connectedness, and it shows.

If you want to commit to the goal of connection and start building a healthy relationship, then you both need to repent for your powerless mindsets and hold yourselves accountable for your own goals in the relationship. Begin to sow generously into your relationship and watch what happens.

God, help us to sow abundantly into our relationship with each other. We want to be connected in a healthy relationship that grows and thrives. Show us where we have missed the mark and help us get back on the right path.

*Are you taking ownership for your part
in achieving the goal of your relationship?*

CROP OF LOVE

"Plant the good seeds of righteousness,
and you will harvest a crop of love.
Plow up the hard ground of your hearts,
for now is the time to seek the LORD,
that he may come
and shower righteousness upon you."

HOSEA 10:12 NLT

At some point in your relationship with your spouse, you both
wanted to be friends. Hopefully, you still do. A great goal for
your marriage is to share a loving, intimate connection with
each other. You should be able to laugh together, to feel safe,
and to be appreciated.

The first step to accomplishing this goal is to agree to pursue
it together. You will need to exchange the skills and habits that
served your old goal of disconnection for skills and habits that
lead you toward connection. It will require a daily reminder to
choose each other. You will need to take responsibility for your
own efforts, attitudes, thoughts, and actions without taking
responsibility for your spouse's. But you can do it, and it will be
worth it.

*Father, thank You for Your love for us. Help us to remember
each day that we can choose each other and make connection a
continual goal. We want to take responsibility for ourselves and for
our part in making that happen. We need Your help to get there.*

*How can you work on creating a loving,
intimate connection with your spouse?*

I LOVE YOU

> "Have I not commanded you? Be strong and courageous.
> Do not be afraid; do not be discouraged,
> for the LORD your God will be with you wherever you go."
>
> JOSHUA 1:9 NIV

You or your spouse may have adopted a protective skill set to pursue your old goal of distance. This may have led to avoiding offerings of vulnerability, such as telling your spouse you love them. In order to establish and work toward a new goal of connection, you will both have to build skills that help you achieve that goal.

Change is difficult and it won't happen immediately, but you can choose to take responsibility for your part in the old goal of distance and move yourself toward connection with your spouse. Put aside all blame and control, face your fear head on, and utter those courageous words your spouse needs to hear: "I love you."

Jesus, we love You. You have told us that we don't need to be afraid because You are with us. Help us to move toward each other without blaming or trying to take control. Forgive us for our lack of love. We want to love like You do.

How hard is it for you to tell your spouse you love them?
How can you move toward connection with your spouse today?

STEADFAST LOVE

The steadfast love of the LORD never ceases;
his mercies never come to an end;
they are new every morning;
great is your faithfulness.

LAMENTATIONS 3:22-23 ESV

Do you know how your spouse best receives love? If you have been trying again and again to send the message of love without receiving a positive result, it will leave you feeling hurt, powerless, and hopeless. You want to be connected to your spouse, but because you cannot seem to repair your disconnect, you may have come to believe that they don't want a connection with you. This feeling of rejection is painful enough to make most people want to change their positive marriage goal from connecting with their spouse to protecting themselves and creating distance.

Is it possible you have misread your spouse's response to your love messages? Or perhaps they have misread your attempts? Could it be that you aren't communicating love in the same language? Take heart; there is a way forward. Be responsible for your part in learning your spouse's language.

God, we want to believe the best about each other, but it can be difficult to get over past hurts and reading through our own filters. Thank You for Your steadfast love and mercy toward us.

Have your attempts to show your spouse love been failing? How can you communicate love effectively?

KEEP FERVENT

Above all, keep fervent in your love for one another,
because love covers a multitude of sins.

1 PETER 4:8 NASB

In his book *The 5 Love Languages,* Gary Chapman describes
categories of behavior used to send and receive the message
of love. Understanding these categories can help you identify
exactly how to create experiences that promote feelings of
connection. Whether intended or not, you and your spouse are
always sending and receiving messages. You are always moving
toward one another or away. The more aware you are of how
you are doing this, the more you can take responsibility for the
messages you send and actively build the connections you want.

The five love languages are Touch, Gifts, Quality Time, Acts of
Service, and Words of Affirmation. Every person usually has
one primary way that they receive and show love. Knowing
someone's love language is as important as knowing what
kind of fuel goes in your car. If you fill a car with the wrong
fuel, it won't be too long before the car breaks down. It's just
as essential to fill your spouse's love tank with the language
they need in order to function and feel connected in your
relationship.

*God, You know exactly how we give and receive love. Teach us
about ourselves and about each other. We want to grow together
in You, remaining fervent in our love.*

*Do you think you know your spouse's love language?
How successful have you been in filling their love tank?*

PHYSICAL TOUCH

Love each other with genuine affection,
and take delight in honoring each other.
ROMANS 12:10 NLT

If you receive love and develop connection through touch, you need physical contact that others may not necessarily need. You likely have a "touch meter" that connects to every other place in your body like a nerve ending. This meter counts the nanoseconds since you were last touched, and as it is depleted by a lack of touch, it registers higher numbers of need. Your anxiety may increase, and you might become easily agitated or aggravated. If your need for affection is starved, you change the way you relate to people. You may disconnect and feel alone even if people are around. But if you get the touch you need, you feel safe, nurtured, and loved.

If your spouse is someone who receives love through touch, you can help them thrive in your relationship and better your connection by filling their love tank with healthy physical affection.

Father, where there is a need for physical touch, show us that. Help us to be sensitive toward each other and to reach outside of our comfort zones to show the kind of love each of us need.

Do either of you need physical touch to fill your love tank? How can you give or receive this kind of love today?

THE RIGHT TOUCH

Let the wise hear and increase in learning,
and the one who understands obtain guidance.

PROVERBS 1:5 ESV

To fill your spouse's love tank with affection, you need to use the right kind of touch. It should be healthy, respectful, and offered as a free gift. Unhealthy, begrudging, or abusive touch will not work. If you want to love a touch person, you need to overcome any fear of touch and learn ways to express healthy affection.

If you are the touch person, you need to learn how to be powerful in communicating your need for touch. Touch is the love language most intrusive to personal space, so those who do not require or even like touch often feel uncomfortable meeting this need. If you can communicate your need clearly, without succumbing to anxiety, then both you and your spouse can move toward one another effectively.

Father, Your wisdom is perfect. Help us learn to love as we listen to each other's needs. You can help us move past the barriers of anxiety and uncertainty in our relationship. Show us what we need to do. We want to learn from You.

*How can you fill or communicate the need
for physical affection today?*

INTENTIONAL ACTS

Put your heart and soul into every activity you do, as though you are doing it for the Lord himself and not merely for others.

COLOSSIANS 3:23 TPT

If showing love to you looks like people doing acts of service, you also have a meter. It marks the ebb and flow of investments into your love bank through the currency of intentional acts of kindness. Every time you enter your home or work environment, the meter begins to run. You scan your surroundings, and your meter is filled or depleted based on what you see. When you see shoes, backpacks, empty dog food bowls, TVs blaring, dirty dishes, office lights left on, copiers with no paper, and other things that need to be fixed, your anxiety climbs. If you are the only person around who needs a high level of order and structure, it can feel as though every mess is your problem to solve—all the time. When these tasks remain chronically undone, you might feel like you're going to lose your mind.

If you are married to someone who receives love through acts of service, you can help them thrive in your relationship and better your connection by noticing and taking care of tasks that are important to them.

God, sometimes there are just so many things to do, and they all feel like chores. Help us to recognize the need for love shown through acts of service and to be willing to participate in it.

Do either of you need acts of service completed to fill your love tank? How can you give or receive this kind of love today?

CONTROL FREAK

Lazy people want much but get little,
but those who work hard will prosper.
PROVERBS 13:4 NLT

If you are an anxiety-filled acts of service person who has just
encountered a messy environment, your initial response is
probably a call for help. If you haven't learned to overcome
your anxiety by communicating effectively, you might start
barking out phrases like, "Really, dishes?", "Doesn't anyone
feed the dog?", "Whose jacket is this?", and "Why are the lights
still on?" Those in the vicinity either ignore the signals, or, if
they feel sufficiently threatened, start to get up and respond.
Although responses help with some of your anxiety, they do
not necessarily fill your love tank. You need to learn how to
sound like a person asking for love, not an angry control freak
requiring the people around you to stop being lazy.

If the acts of service person is your spouse, fill their love tank
by finding out what they need and doing it as a free act of
love, not coercion. The simplest of tasks can go a long way to
making them feel loved and strengthen your connection.

*Jesus, please calm our anxieties and help us communicate clearly
and kindly with each other, so we can help demonstrate love in
the way it is best received.*

How can you fill or communicate the need for acts of service today?

TOKEN OF LOVE

Every good and perfect gift is from above, coming down from the Father of the heavenly lights, who does not change like shifting shadows.
JAMES 1:17 NIV

Gifts people constantly soak up evidence that the people in their lives know them and think about them even when they are not around. This evidence lies in a physical token of love. If you are a gift person, you hear, feel, and experience love through the offering of a gift that says someone knows you and has been paying attention to you.

If your spouse is a gifts person, they will probably speak in the language of gifts to you. They celebrate special moments to commemorate the relationship. Anniversaries, birthdays, holidays, and just about any other occasion provide them with reasons for giving gifts. You can bet that they have paid attention to what you like to do, what you like to eat, what you collect, or where you've been in the world. Their gifts to you will symbolize this attention to the details of your life, and they will expect you to reciprocate in kind. You can help your spouse thrive in your relationship and better your connection by paying attention to what they like and giving small tokens of your love in the form of gifts.

Heavenly Father, You know us perfectly. Help us to learn each other well enough to know what the best offering of love would be.

Do either of you need gifts to fill your love tank?
How can you give or receive this kind of love today?

GOOD GIFTS

"If you sinful people know how to give good gifts to your children, how much more will your heavenly Father give good gifts to those who ask him."

MATTHEW 7:1 NLT

Whoever coined the phrase, "It's the thought that counts," was definitely a gifts person. The gift says far more than a price tag; the thought behind it is valued more than the cost because that's what makes the gift a symbol of devotion. If you receive love through gifts, the driving question of your heart is if others really know you. Are you on their mind?

If you are married to a gifts person, don't forget to bring a gift to a special occasion, and don't give them something without a lot of thought. You don't want to send the message that you aren't thinking about them or that you don't pay attention to them. Do the work required to find a gift that says, "You were on my mind. I thought you'd like this," and fill their love tank.

Father, You think about us all the time, and Your gift-giving is unmatched. Thank You for Your devotion to us. Help us to be mindful of each other and to send a message of love and importance to one another.

How can you fill or communicate the need for gifts today?

ACTIVE INTEREST

My beloved spoke and said to me,
"Arise my darling,
my beautiful one, come with me."
SONG OF SOLOMON 2:10 NIV

If you feel love and connection when people find you interesting, meaning they want to be with you, you are a quality time person. When you invite someone to have a conversation or join you in an activity, you want their response to send a message that they are interested in you. Your anxiety levels are reduced, and you feel connected when others choose to be with you, listen to you, and ask questions that make you feel cared for.

If your spouse needs quality time, make it a habit to give them your whole focus and full attention when they share. Create an environment where they feel free to share what is going on in their lives. Your active interest will fill their love tank.

God, You are so interested in us. You desire to be with us. You are always listening, always engaged when we talk to You. Help us to walk by Your example and show interest in each other. We want to be attentive and compassionate when we are together.

Do either of you need quality time to fill your love tank? How can you give or receive this kind of love today?

A QUIET PLACE

Then Jesus said, "Let's go off by ourselves to a quiet place
and rest awhile." He said this because there were so many
people coming and going that Jesus and his apostles didn't
even have time to eat.
So they left by boat for a quiet place,
where they could be alone.

MARK 6:31-32 NLT

If you need quality time, pain probably enters the relationship
for you when you don't feel like you are being listened to. If
your spouse doesn't make time to fully engage with you and
doesn't pay attention to you, it sends a message that they are
not interested in you, or, even worse, that you aren't important.

If you are married to a quality time person, remember that the
amount of time isn't necessarily what matters. It isn't quantity;
it's quality. Your spouse needs genuine interest and engagement
from you. This is what determines the quality of the time spent.
Engage in an activity or conversation with all your energy and
attention, at the deepest possible level. This will cause them to
thrive in the relationship and to feel better connected with you.

*God, sometimes we need a quiet place together to rest. Would You
help us find that? Encourage us to spend quality time together,
listening to and engaging with each other. Being together is a good
way to connect, and we recognize the need for it.*

How can you fill or communicate the need for quality time today?

INTENT OF WORDS

Never let ugly or hateful words come from your mouth, but instead let your words become beautiful gifts that encourage others; do this by speaking words of grace to help them.

EPHESIANS 4:29 TPT

The spirit or intent of words exchanged impacts words of affirmation people powerfully. They feel most enjoyed and appreciated when words and body language include a positive tone of voice, facial expressions, and word choice. Anxiety rises and falls with the way words are used in conversation. A simple word of encouragement creates safety and connection. Love flows into them with every positive word, and they relax as they experience someone verbally expressing enjoyment in them. Conversely, when the tone of a conversation or interaction turns negative or critical, the anxiety level begins to climb and hurt is inevitable.

To make your spouse feel loved, speak words of affirmation over them. This language will help them feel better connected and like they don't need to defend themselves, withdraw, or become verbally hostile.

Father, many times the words we speak are not encouraging or kind. Forgive us for when we have torn each other down with careless words. Help us to speak words of grace and love instead.

Do either of you need words of affirmation to fill your love tank? How can you give or receive this kind of love today?

Timely Words

Timely advice is lovely,
like golden apples in a silver basket.
To one who listens, valid criticism
is like a gold earring or other gold jewelry.

PROVERBS 25:11-12 NLT

How do you give correction or constructive criticism to someone who needs words of affirmation to fill their love tank? You use the hero sandwich. These sandwiches have twice as much "I love you" as they do criticism. The bread is the nice, positive, reinforcing words of affirmation that communicate your love, and the meat is the constructive criticism. Begin and end the conversation with words of affirmation. *I love you. You are important to me.*

If you use the hero sandwich with your spouse, the positive "I love you" messages at the beginning and end drive down anxiety and create safety even though you are communicating that you are upset. This approach allows honest, open relationships to form with your spouse who might otherwise shut down in the face of critical feedback.

Jesus, You knew how to speak love to all kinds of different people. You knew how to offer correction and guidance without cutting people down personally. We want to learn from You and approach situations the way You did—with love. Give us wisdom to communicate well.

*How can you fill or communicate the need
for words of affirmation today?*

FULL BLAST

Just as you excel in everything, in faith, speaking, knowledge, and in all earnestness and in the love we inspired in you, see that you also excel in this gracious work.

2 CORINTHIANS 8:7 NASB

When you know how to speak each other's language, it will help you feel more connected. Communicating becomes easier when you seek to understand how your spouse is feeling and what they are thinking during your conversation. This way, you can keep your love flowing while you work out misunderstandings and conflicts.

As a couple, one of your biggest tasks is to learn how to reduce the disconnection and increase the connection between you. Then the atmosphere of your home and your relationships with others in your home will improve. Turn your love on full blast and chase away the destructive forces of fear and anxiety!

Father, help us to speak the language of love to each other. You are kind, and good, and full of wisdom. We look to You today to be our source. We need You to work in and through us, so we can rightly demonstrate Your love.

How are you seeking to understand each other during your conversations?

RELATIONAL TOOLS

Listen to advice and accept instruction,
that you may gain wisdom in the future.
PROVERBS 19:20 ESV

What is the goal in your relationship? Are you trying to create a safe connection or a safe distance? Are you building a skill set to move away from or control the distance between you and your spouse? Or are you building a skill set to move toward them and keep your love on no matter what?

Until you commit to the goal of connection, all the relational tools in the world are not going to help you. It's only when you decide to take responsibility to pursue connection that you will discover why you need tools. It's only when you commit to moving toward someone that you will seek the knowledge and skills necessary to reach them.

Jesus, we want to be committed to the goal of connection in our marriage. We need Your relational tools. Holy Spirit, help us in our pursuit to move toward each other. Give us the grace to love well.

Do you see your need for tools in your pursuit of connecting with your spouse?

A HEART BATTLE

There is no fear in love, but perfect love casts out fear.
For fear has to do with punishment, and whoever fears
has not been perfected in love.

1 JOHN 4:18 ESV

The choice to pursue the goal of connection will bring you right up against the real conflict that lies at the core of every relationship. It is a spiritual battle—a heart battle—drawn between the two most powerful forces that drive us: fear and love.

If you want to be powerful people capable of building an intimate relationship, then it is absolutely vital that you learn how these forces operate and align yourselves with love. God is perfect love, and in Him, you are capable of loving without fear. When He is present in your relationship, you give your love the opportunity of being perfected.

God, You are the author of love. There is no fear in You. We want to learn how to operate in a spirit of love and reject the spirit of fear. Be at the center of our relationship so we can build it the right way—on love, not fear.

How do fear and love battle for control in your relationship?

YOU HAVE A CHOICE

Don't you realize that grace frees you to choose your own master? But choose carefully, for you surrender yourself to become a servant—bound to the one you choose to obey. If you choose to love sin, it will become your master, and it will own you and reward you with death. But if you choose to love and obey God, he will lead you into perfect righteousness.

ROMANS 6:16 TPT

What will you do with the choice to keep your love on? You do have a choice. You can turn it on, or you can turn it off. If you turn it off, which is your choice, you have to accept responsibility for turning it off. It doesn't turn off by itself, and no one else turns it off for you. No one else can turn it back on except you.

If you feel like your relationship goal is safe distance from each other, it's time for you to figure out how to turn your love back on. You both have to take responsibility for your part in the relationship and start creating ways to build connection and togetherness. It will take work.

God, the choice to love does not come easily or naturally every day. It is sometimes the most difficult choice we will have to make in a day. Help us to turn on our love. Teach us how to build connection. Thank You for Your grace that has freed us to choose the right thing.

How can you choose to turn your love back on if you recognize it is off?

CONNECTION GOAL

"I am the vine; you are the branches.
If you remain in me and I in you, you will bear much fruit;
apart from me you can do nothing."
JOHN 15:5 NIV

You and your spouse will begin to experience love when your goal is connection. If your goal is to create safe distance, that's easy. You don't need help doing that. But you will not find marital satisfaction or intimacy in distance. A goal that makes you pursue each other and move toward each other even when you are hurt or disconnected requires each of you to take responsibility for your part.

Whatever you decide is your choice and your responsibility. But if you want to work on creating connection with each other, you have to identify whether one or both of you have turned your love off. You have to be willing to ask the hard questions and choose to keep your love on, or turn it back on, whatever the case may be.

Father, in You we can grow together and begin to bear good fruit. Without You, there is no way we can choose love and connection. You are love. Help us to pursue each other even when we are hurt. We want to abide in You and keep our love on.

How can you pursue a goal of connection today?

GREATEST COMMANDMENT

"Teacher, which is the greatest commandment in the Law?"
Jesus replied: "'Love the Lord your God with all your heart and
with all your soul and with all your mind. This is the first and
greatest commandment. And the second is like it: 'Love your
neighbor as yourself.'"

MATTHEW 22:36-39 NIV

When the Pharisee asked Jesus what the greatest
commandment was, he was looking for a rule. Jesus essentially
said, "Just love." This is the greatest part of your life. The
greatest thing you could be doing is choosing to keep your
love on. It creates a place for God to work through. For the
kingdom of heaven to reign in your relationship, you do your
part by keeping your love on.

Jesus goes on to say that there is no greater thing you can do
for someone else than to lay down your life. This is what makes
you the MVP in your relationship: you are willing to lay your
life down, which means it doesn't have to be all about you all
the time. As a matter of fact, this is a part of you choosing your
spouse in a relationship. You keep your love on even if they
have turned theirs off.

*Jesus, Your commandment to love feels like it should be easy, but
it is the opposite! Show us how to love like You never turn Your
love off. We want to love You and each other in a way that is
pleasing to You.*

*How do you see the greatest commandment
working in your relationship?*

HOW TO LOVE

This is how we can be sure that we love the children of God: by having a passionate love for God and by obedience to his commands.

1 JOHN 5:2 TPT

Maybe you shut your love off because you thought that would help you defend yourself. What actually happens is that you become full of anxiety. When you turn off love, fear replaces it. And fear has its work in you because you turned your love off. If you keep your love on, you have something Jesus can get a hold of.

When you decide your relationship goal should be connection, you need to turn your love on and discover again how your spouse feels love. What do they need to fill their tanks? Can you remember? Did you ever know? When there is a lack of connection, it's a pipeline for anxiety. Cut that off by figuring out how to love each other in the way you both receive it.

God, we know that in order to love each other, we must first love You. Show us how to turn our love for each other back on. Guide us in the right way to fill our individual love tanks. We say no to anxiety and fear ruling our relationship, and we say yes to Your love.

What is the best way for you to show your spouse love in a way they will receive it?

THE BEST YOU

God has not given us a spirit of fear and timidity,
but of power, love, and self-discipline.
2 TIMOTHY 1:7 NLT

When you have a strategy to increase love in a relationship, that same strategy is decreasing fear. When you send your spouse a message that says, "I love you," and it sinks in and they feel love, fear is dissipating from the relationship. The very best you shows up when you feel loved.

Conversely, the very worst you shows up when you feel afraid. When you and your spouse are disconnected, fear increases. The remedy is to get the connection back—to drive the fear away so the best people show up in the relationship again. When you learn how your spouse receives love, practice it until it becomes a habit.

God, You have not given us the spirit of fear. We choose not to buy into it or side with it any longer. You give us power, love, and a sound mind that can help us make the right decisions toward love and connection.

Who is showing up in your relationship right now:
the best you or the worst you?

BECOME FLUENT

I suppose that the world has all sorts of languages,
and each conveys meaning to the ones who speak it.
1 CORINTHIANS 14:10 TPT

Becoming fluent in another language takes time and energy.
If the language your spouse receives love in is not the same
language you speak, you need to study and practice! It's not
impossible to learn a new language, but it won't happen by
itself, and it won't happen overnight. Start the journey toward
each other by becoming students of your spouse's language.

If they are touch communicators, they need affection. Touch
has a powerful effect on them; if they have enough of it, they'll
be fine. If your spouse loves acts of service, learn how to help
them. Don't act like you are being controlled by their need;
rather, notice what they feel needs to be done and do it. Give
your gifts person something that shows you know what they
like and that you were thinking about them when you weren't
together. Spend time engaging in an activity that your quality
time person enjoys. Be present and be interested. Tell your
words person how much they mean to you. Speak words of
love and life. As you become fluent in each other's language,
your connection will deepen.

*Father, You are the language master! We ask You to teach us
the language of love that will resonate best with each person
we come into contact with.*

*What one step can you take toward learning
your spouse's language?*

INCREASED LOVE

If we love one another, God abides in us
and his love is perfected in us.
1 JOHN 4:12 ESV

One of the most effective things to create better connection is to drive down fear and increase the love. As you work on being connected, fear dissipates. Both people in the relationship get effective messages from each other as love is expressed in the language best received for each person.

Together, you will begin to communicate "I care about us" messages. You are both saying, "I choose to keep my love on. I choose us. I value our relationship. I love you." To the success that you bring that message, you drive fear away. The chances of you both experiencing love increases by keeping your love on.

God, we love You. We confess our need for Your love to be perfected in us, so we can rightly love one another. Help us to continue to pursue love and say no to fear.

How can you drive down fear in your relationship today?

REACTION TO PAIN

Our momentary, light affliction is producing for us an eternal weight of glory far beyond all comparison.

2 CORINTHIANS 4:17 NASB

How is it that two people who vowed to love and care for one another for a lifetime end up slowly moving away from one another, until the goal and practices of disconnection become entrenched in their relationship? Do people just decide one day to stop loving one another?

The answer, sadly, is yes. But it's usually not a conscious decision. Most often it is a reaction to pain or the fear of pain. Pain teaches us to react from the moment we enter the earth. The first reaction we have to pain is to cry. As newborns, when someone bigger responds to our cries by doing something to make us feel better, we learn that crying is a helpful reaction to pain or discomfort.

Father, where we have chosen to walk away from our love, we ask for forgiveness. We don't want to react out of our pain; instead, we want to be mindful of eternity and what is in store for us beyond life's afflictions. Your glory is worth every painful thing we have walked through.

How has a reaction to pain caused you to distance yourselves from each other?

PERSEVERANCE THROUGH PAIN

We also glory in our sufferings,
because we know that suffering produces perseverance;
perseverance, character; and character, hope.

ROMANS 5:3-4 NIV

As you grow up, your reactions teach you how to avoid pain. As a child, even though your parents told you not to do something, you often had to satisfy your own curiosity, which likely didn't end well. The iron really was hot, gloves actually kept your fingers warm, and chasing siblings around the house did end with fingers slammed in the door.

Very quickly, you realize that certain situations produce something bad, something painful. Once you learn that, your behavior around those situations is instinctively driven by the goal of pain avoidance. While this is good and healthy, pain avoidance can multiply and bleed into many areas, leading some to live in constant fear and miss out on experiences that are produced by persevering through the pain.

God, rather than running to avoid pain, help us to persevere. Our hope is in You and in the life that lays beyond the grave. Help us to respond to each other in love instead of giving in to fear.

Do you avoid pain at all costs, or can you see the benefit of perseverance in certain areas?

HUMAN INSTINCT

Good sense is a fountain of life to him who has it,
but the instruction of fools is folly.
PROVERBS 16:22 ESV

Human beings generally develop three classic reactions to the threat of pain: fight, flight, or freeze. All of these reactions have the same goal—distance! You want to get away from scary things that can hurt you.

You probably haven't been bitten by a rattlesnake, but you know what would happen if you were. Because of the danger, very few people keep pet rattlesnakes in their homes. People who handle rattlesnakes do so with instruments of protection and control such as cages, prods, guns, and gloves. No one is looking to create a loving, lasting, intimate relationship with a rattlesnake. It's a basic human instinct—when the threat of harm is high, the level of love is low.

God, help us to view our relationship with the lens of Your love. We don't want to run from each other, fight, or freeze. We want to move toward each other and create a relationship full of light and joy. Instruct us in Your wisdom.

How do you typically respond to the threat of pain?

RATTLESNAKE RELATIONSHIP

My child, never forget the things I have taught you.
Store my commands in your heart.
If you do this, you will live many years,
and your life will be satisfying.

PROVERBS 3:1-2 NLT

Relationships with people are a lot more complicated than relationships with rattlesnakes. People offer both comfort and protection from pain as well as the threat of pain. The mom who fed you in response to your cries is also the one who yelled at you, the dad who taught you to ride a bike is also the one who could never tell you he loved you, and the spouse who promised you unconditional love is the person who could break your heart with rejection and betrayal.

The question is, how you will react to the pain you experience in relationships? If you fall back on the classic fear-driven reactions, you will start treating people like rattlesnakes by running away or trying to control them, so they won't hurt you. Neither of these options will help you pursue and protect the goal of connection in a relationship.

Father, we come to You with our hurt and pain. You comfort us and love us back to wholeness. Help us to remember what You have taught us. You are near, and You are good. We look to You to help us with our goal of connection.

How do you react to the pain you experience in relationships?

CONTROLLING BEHAVIORS

We have been rescued from our enemies
so we can serve God without fear,
in holiness and righteousness
for as long as we live.
LUKE 1:74-75 NLT

Unfortunately, many people grow up in relational cultures that use rattlesnake tools to deal with pain and the fear of pain—tools that control, manipulate, remove freedom, threaten, and withhold love. The message is that pain will occur if you do not let yourself be controlled. This creates powerlessness.

When parents give appropriate consequences to children to help them learn how to avoid harm, that is healthy. Parents who try to make their child's choices for them and punish them when they don't comply, teach their children to be powerless. Children quickly learn that they need to surrender control if they don't want the most powerful adult in their life to get mad, withhold love, or hurt them in some way. As they develop adult relationships, they believe the lie that drives the cycle of fear, control, punishment, and disconnection. Unless they repent from this lie, they cannot help but bring controlling behaviors into their relationships as well.

God, show us where we have brought lies into our relationship from the way we were brought up. Help us to have grace for each other.

How can you eliminate controlling behaviors in your relationship with your spouse?

NEW TOOLS

In righteousness you will be established:
Tyranny will be far from you;
you will have nothing to fear.
Terror will be far removed;
it will not come near you.

ISAIAH 54:14 NIV

Plenty of people grow up saying they are never going to be like their parents. You may have said it yourself a time or two. Yet, the first time you run into a scary or painful relational situation, you find yourself spouting out the same exact words, making the same faces, and dragging around the same manipulative, fear-inflicting tools that once caused you so much pain.

You have probably tried to learn new relational tools, but the minute you get scared, your real beliefs are unmasked. In the face of pain, you align yourself with the goal of fear—distance, control, and punishment. Be encouraged; it is possible to break out of these habits and develop healthy responses to fear and pain. You can start by identifying your reactions and practicing how to choose love.

Father God, we need Your help to break the cycle of unhealthy responses to fear and pain. Show us what it means to choose love when we feel afraid. We want to surround ourselves with Your peace and use Your wisdom to change the way we react to unwanted circumstances.

How can you develop healthy responses to fear and pain?

COMFORT ZONE

If there is any encouragement in Christ, if any consolation of love,
if any fellowship of the Spirit, if any affection and compassion,
make my joy complete by being of the same mind, maintaining
the same love, united in spirit, intent on one purpose.

PHILIPPIANS 2:1-2 NASB

Fear-based reactions to pain are instinctive, which means
that they operate at a very different level in your brain than
conscious, rational choices. You execute them without
thinking. And because they come so naturally, they seem
normal.

One expression of this natural, fear-based human normal is
that you tend to surround yourself with people who feel safe.
Safe people are those who agree with you and reinforce what
you already believe about the world. When you get around
someone who doesn't support your worldview, it usually
triggers your defenses. Whether you know it or not, your brain
tells you that you don't want to be around that person because
they make you uncomfortable. It's human nature to maintain
your comfort zone.

*God, it's easy to be around people who see things the same way
we do. Give us grace to respond to those who don't support our
worldview with love and patience. Help us to be united where it
matters, and let unimportant things go.*

*Do you and your spouse see eye-to-eye on most things?
How is your comfort zone challenged?*

DIFFERENT PEOPLE

We no longer see each other in our former state—
Jew or non-Jew, rich or poor, male or female—
because we're all one through our union with Jesus Christ.

GALATIANS 3:28 TPT

As natural as it is, the fear-based normal of surrounding yourselves with only people who agree with you is a major problem. Instinctive reactions to pain do not bring out the best in human beings.

When we apply this to a social level, we find oppression, injustice, racism, war, etc. Most social evils can be traced back to the instinctive fear of people who are different. Societies are created that eliminate or marginalize those people who are different, so others feel safe. On a personal level, fear-based reactions cause most misunderstandings and hurt in relationships.

God, we can see how reactions based in fear do not lead to good connection in relationships. They bring about further hurt and separation. Help us to see each other as equals and to treat each other as You treated those around You, choosing love above everything else.

What fear-based reactions cause misunderstandings in your relationship with each other? How about in your relationships with others?

RESPONSE ABILITY

Reckless words are like the thrusts of a sword,
cutting remarks meant to stab and to hurt.
But the words of the wise soothe and heal.
PROVERBS 12:18 TPT

If you want to preserve your relationship, then you must learn to respond instead of react to fear and pain. Responding does not come naturally. You can react without thinking, but you cannot respond without training your mind to think, your will to choose, and your body to obey. It is precisely this training that brings the best qualities—courage, empathy, reason, compassion, justice, and generosity—to the surface.

The ability to exercise these qualities and respond gives you other options besides disconnection in the face of relational pain. Powerful people are not slaves to their instincts. They can respond with love in the face of pain and fear. This "response-ability" is essential to building healthy relationships.

Creator God, You know how we are made. You know what comes naturally and what doesn't. Reckless words are too easy to throw around, and they are so damaging to relationships. Teach us how to respond to fear with words and actions that are kind and soothing.

How can you begin training yourselves to respond to each other with love?

FREE TO LOVE

You, my brothers and sisters, were called to be free.
But do not use your freedom to indulge the flesh;
rather, serve one another humbly in love.

GALATIANS 5:13 NIV

In order to begin training yourself to respond in love, the first thing you need to accept is that you cannot control other people. The only person you can control—on a good day—is yourself. This is a fundamental principle of human freedom. You were designed to be free, to make choices, to love.

God put two trees in the Garden of Eden and gave mankind a choice. Without choice, you don't have freedom, and more importantly, you don't have love. Love requires freedom. God chose you, loves you, and wants you to choose Him and love Him in return.

God, thank You for the freedom You have given us. You allow us to choose a relationship with You and with each other. Help us to use our freedom to serve each other and to experience the gift of love.

How does your freedom to choose give you
the opportunity to experience love?

NOT CONTROLLED

"I have loved you with an everlasting love;
I have drawn you with unfailing kindness."

JEREMIAH 31:3 NIV

God gave us a free choice even though it meant risking rejection and the devastation of a disconnected relationship. The tragedy of the Fall actually proclaims that He does not want to control us. He didn't control us in the Garden, and He doesn't control us now. Many people find this difficult to believe.

If you were raised with a powerless, fear-driven mindset based on the belief that you can control people and they can control you, then you will naturally perceive God as a controlling punisher. You will take the laws of the Old Testament—all the verses and stories about wrath, judgment, and the fear of the Lord—and conclude that God wants to control us, and we need to be controlled. Our hearts are desperately wicked, and we can't be trusted, so God uses the threat of punishment to maintain the distance between us and Him.

Everlasting God, You have loved us from the beginning, and You will love us until the end. Thank You that You do not control us; rather, You give us the ability to choose You. Your kindness draws us in, and Your love keeps us close. We choose You today.

*Do you perceive God as controlling and distant?
How can you change your perspective of Him?*

PASSIONATE PURSUIT

His love broke open the way,
and he brought me into a beautiful, broad place.
He rescued me—because his delight is in me!

PSALM 18:19 TPT

The Bible doesn't show us a God who is pursuing the goal of distance between Himself and a bunch of scary sinners. Instead, it reveals a God who is relentlessly closing that distance and paying the ultimate price to repair the disconnection we created in our relationship.

God's number one goal with you is connection, and nothing—neither pain nor death—will prevent Him from moving toward you and responding to you with love. His perfect love for you is absolutely fearless. He is not afraid of you, and He never will be. You can make the goal of your marriage the same: connection without fear.

Father, You have pursued us with love and delight that go beyond our ability to imagine. Thank You for creating a way for us to have closeness with You. You continue to close the distance between us through Your Son, Jesus. Help us to move toward each other in our relationship and work on removing fear.

Do you believe that God is passionate about pursuing you?

FILLED WITH FREEDOM

The Lord is the Spirit,
and where the Spirit of the Lord is,
there is freedom.

2 CORINTHIANS 3:17 ESV

God's message to you is that He loves you no matter what. He is not afraid of your mistakes, and you don't have to be afraid of them either. Other people's mistakes don't need to scare you. They may be painful because many things in life are, but pain and the fear of pain no longer have the power to control you. You are always free to choose.

What are you going to do? Remember that God is always there for you whatever you choose. He continually moves toward you in love, giving you the choice to love Him in return. He never takes your choices away. The more God fills your life, the more freedom you will have.

God, thank You for Your love. You embrace us when we fail, and You continue to give us freedom to fail again and again. We want to love You in return. We want to know Your fullness in our lives. We choose to be bound to You in love no matter what circumstances we face or mistakes we make.

What is your freedom-filled choice today?

BREAK THE CYCLE

Our struggle is not against flesh and blood, but against the rulers,
against the powers, against the world forces of this darkness,
against spiritual forces of wickedness in the heavenly places.

EPHESIANS 6:12 NASB

God is not afraid of sin or sinners, but most of us are. We're
afraid of people's mistakes, and we're afraid of our own. It's no
wonder our entire society, including our court system, is set up
in such a way that fear and punishment are the solutions to bad
behavior. As long as we operate out of fear, we will inevitably
continue to reproduce distance and disconnection in our
relationships with God, others, and ourselves.

The cycle can only be broken by repenting from the lie that
you can control other people and by accepting the truth that
you must control yourself. As soon as you begin to believe this
truth and stop trying to control people, you will be confronted
with a lot of resistance from the old normal. It won't give way
to heaven's normal without a fight.

*God, we need Your help. We want to create a good connection,
but we admit at times we are afraid. Give us the courage to
believe that we can each control ourselves. Fight with us against
the cycles that create distance. We know our struggle is not
against each other but against things unseen. Go before us
and lead us into victory!*

Are you and your spouse ready to battle against the old normal?

WHOLE ARMOR

Put on all the whole armor of God,
that you may be able to stand against the schemes of the devil.

EPHESIANS 6:11 ESV

When you turn from the goal of distance to the goal of connection, don't be surprised if you or your spouse (or both of you) are plunged into a battle against fear. Fear and love are enemies. They come from two opposing kingdoms. Fear comes from the devil, who would like nothing more than to keep you permanently disconnected and isolated. Love comes from God, who is always working to heal and restore your connection with Him and other people. He wants to bring you into healthy, life-giving relationships.

Fear and love have opposite agendas and opposite strategies for achieving them. They cannot coexist in a person, relationship, or culture. You can stand ready for the battle against fear when you put on your God-given armor of love.

Heavenly Father, we align ourselves with Your kingdom today. You give us what we need to stand and fight the plans of the enemy. Teach us how to put on our armor so we are ready for battle. Thank You for Your love that covers and protects us as we war against fear.

How can you use love to battle fear today?

NO ADHERENCE POLICY

The Spirit you received does not make you slaves, so that you live in fear again; rather, the Spirit you received brought about your adoption to sonship. And by him we cry, "Abba, Father."

ROMANS 8:15 NIV

God is very clear that the Spirit He put in you is not the spirit of fear, but the Spirit of love. This Spirit gives you power, love, and a sound mind (See 2 Timothy 1:7.). God is also clear that partnering with the Spirit of love is the way to displace fear in your life. "There is no fear in love. But perfect love casts out fear, because fear has to do with punishment. The one who fears is not made perfect in love" (1 John 4:18).

If you want to partner with the Holy Spirit, then you must have a strict no-tolerance policy about fear and punishment in your life and relationships. It doesn't matter how long you've used those tools—they have to go!

Holy Spirit of love, we join with You today. We throw away our old tools that created distance and pick up Your tools of love, grace, and patience. We determine to stand together and fight for our relationship. We declare our freedom from fear and adoption into Your family of love.

How can you get rid of your old tools and take up the new?

Choose a Partner

"Counsel and sound judgment are mine;
I have insight, I have power."

PROVERBS 8:14 NIV

Learning to partner with the Spirit of love requires you to become powerful. This is a serious challenge. When Paul told Timothy that the Spirit of love is also the Spirit of power and a sound mind, he implied that its opposite, the spirit of fear, is the spirit of powerlessness and a weak, divided mind.

When you grow up partnering with the spirit of fear, as most do, you learn to simply hand over your brain and your power, letting fear take control. But as soon as you decide to partner with the Spirit of love, you have to think and make powerful choices. To turn your love back on, you have to marshal your internal resources to think, decide, and act. You become powerful and exercise self-control so you can say, "Yes, I love my spouse."

God, You have given us all the wisdom we need in Your Word. Your counsel is good. Your Word is truth. Thank You for the insight that comes when we spend time reading it. Help us to encourage each other with Scripture; let it wash over us and renew us.

How will you partner with the Spirit of love today?

IT IS POSSIBLE

"Humanly speaking, it is impossible.
But with God everything is possible."
MATTHEW 19:26 NLT

Sometimes the choice you make to turn your love on later in marriage is more powerful than the choice you made to get married in the first place. The choice to love after experiencing a history of pain is a very difficult one.

You know that your choice to love cannot be conditioned by what your spouse does or doesn't do. You know that choosing love has to be strong enough to withstand the fear and pain that may have derailed you in the past. After years of experiencing pain in relationships, you understand how powerful you need to be to make the choice of love. But you can do it. With God, all things are possible.

God, we admit that sometimes it feels impossible to choose love. But You are love and You choose us over and over again in spite of our sin and weakness. We say together that we believe we can choose each other. We can choose to turn our love on and keep it on because You are behind our choice, and that makes it possible.

How can you make the powerful choice to love today?

RETURN ON INVESTMENT

By the grace of God I am what I am, and his grace to me was not without effect. No, I worked harder than all of them— yet not I, but the grace of God that was with me.

1 CORINTHIANS 15:10 NIV

Do you want to win the battle between fear and love in your relationship? You can start by making two fundamental commitments. First, remember it's your job to control yourself; you don't get to control other people. Second, your number one goal and priority is to build and protect connection.

These commitments are among the most powerful choices you can make, and they will require more of you than anything you can imagine. But the person you will become, and the relationship you will be capable of experiencing together as a result, are absolutely worth the investment.

Jesus, thank You for Your grace that helps us fight for connection. Teach us how to build it and protect it. Give us strength to control ourselves and not others. Show us how to invest heavily in our marriage especially when things are difficult.

What is your return on investment in your relationship with your spouse?

BEST-KEPT SECRET

"People are known in this same way. Out of the virtue stored in their hearts, good and upright people will produce good fruit. Likewise, out of the evil hidden in their hearts, evil ones will produce what is evil. For the overflow of what has been stored in your heart will be seen by your fruit and will be heard in your words."

LUKE 6:45 TPT

After making the commitments to control yourself only and to pursue connection, you will need to acquire several skill sets in order to follow through with them. It begins with being able to communicate love consistently in ways that your spouse can hear and receive.

It may sound simple, but if you have grown up in a fear-based, love-starved relational culture, it can be revolutionary to break the silence and start actively communicating what has been one of your best-kept secrets: "I love you. My relationship with you is really important to me."

Jesus, we look to Your example and see how terribly far short we fall of loving like You loved. Help us to put in the hard work that produces good fruit in our relationship. We want our love for each other to not only be lodged in our hearts and minds, but to also overflow from our mouths.

Can you communicate the importance of your relationship to your spouse today?

JUST SAY IT

Gracious words are like a honeycomb,
sweetness to the soul and health to the body.
PROVERBS 16:24 ESV

Do you or your spouse have a parent who wouldn't or couldn't say, "I love you"? If the answer is yes, you may find that you have spent your entire life blowing off that glaring omission, trying to accept by faith that your mother or father really loved you. You might make excuses for them, saying you know they loved you, they just had a hard time saying it.

Inner healing is necessary in these situations because a parent's silence on the topic of love allows anxiety to persist in your relationships and weakens your connections. The pain of this disconnection wreaks havoc on your wellbeing—mentally, emotionally, spiritually, and even physically. If you want to cast out all the fear in your relationships, then you need to leave no room for doubt in people's minds and hearts that you truly love them.

Father, without You there is no such thing as love. Help us to forgive those in our lives who haven't been able to verbally express their love for us. We recognize the need for that kind of communication, and we commit to making it a priority in our relationship.

Who do you need to tell that you love them today?

BEST SELF FORWARD

Hatred stirs up strife,
But love covers all offenses.
PROVERBS 10:12 NASB

It's amazing how much you can strengthen a relational connection and resolve relational problems by simply speaking in one another's love languages. People who are afraid are bound to show you their worst. People who feel loved, on the other hand, will usually show you their best.

When you begin to speak your spouse's language, each display of love, no matter how seemingly small, is a powerful act of spiritual warfare that removes anxiety from the environment, replaces it with freedom and safety, and invites them to bring their best self forward in the relationship.

Thank You, God, that no matter how terribly we act toward You, You still love us. You love us in our darkest moments. Help us to show each other the kind of love that covers weakness and offense. We want to bring our best selves to this relationship.

How can you help your spouse bring their best self forward?

ADJUSTMENTS

Take control of what I say, O LORD,
and guard my lips.
PSALM 141:3 NLT

As you manage your love toward each other and pursue the
goal of connection, you will need feedback so you can both
understand how you're affecting each other and identify where
you need to make adjustments.

Healthy communication requires that you provide your spouse
with honest, relevant information about how their behavior
is affecting your life. It's not about judging them or telling
them how they need to change. It is about trusting them to
do whatever they need to do to protect and nourish your
connection and letting them know that you will do the same.

*God, You desire honesty spoken in love. It can be hard to talk
about our relationship, especially when we need to share things
that aren't going well. Give us the grace to speak honorably with
each other and about each other. Help our communication to be
done with truth and gentleness.*

*What adjustments do you both need to make in
your attempt to pursue your goal of connection?*

THE REAL TEST

"I will instruct you and teach you in the way you should go,
I will counsel you with my eye upon you."
PSALM 32:8 ESV

God practices healthy communication with you. In the verse above, God says He will instruct and teach you, and He will guide you with His eye. This sounds a little strange at first. How is God going to lead you with His eyeball? He can't control you with His eyeball, and that's the point.

What God can do with His eye is show you how He feels about the choices you're making and how they're affecting His heart. Eyes are the windows to the heart. When God shows you how your choices affect His heart and your connection with Him, you get to choose how you will respond to the information. Will you adjust, if necessary, in order to protect your connection with Him? That is the real test of a healthy relationship.

God, we want to please Your heart. We want to listen to Your counsel and walk in the ways You want us to walk. Help us to be ready to listen when You talk. Give us ears to hear and hearts to understand what You are saying. We know You want what's best for us.

What is God communicating with you about your choices?

BATTLE PLAN

Put on the full armor of God, so that when the day of evil comes, you may be able to stand your ground, and after you have done everything, to stand.

EPHESIANS 6:13 NIV

In order to control yourself and pursue the goal of connection, you need a new plan for dealing with the things that threaten your connections. You need to have a punishment-free, control-free, fear-free plan for dealing with people who make mistakes, engaging in conflict, and setting healthy boundaries.

Your success in this plan is fully determined by how powerful you are willing to become. Will you become a person who can keep your love on, no matter what? A powerful person says, "I am going to be okay no matter what you do. You can hurt me, but you cannot make me turn my love off. I am relentlessly going to do what I have to do to protect my connection with you, no matter what." When you can say and do this in the face of fear, mistakes, and pain, you have already won the battle between fear and love.

God, give us the courage to love no matter what. We need Your help to pursue connection with each other and to fight for our relationship even when it feels one-sided. We take up the armor You have given us, and we choose to stand.

How powerful are you willing to become?

WHICH KINGDOM

The Kingdom of God is not just a lot of talk;
it is living by God's power.

1 CORINTHIANS 4:29 NLT

Choosing to move toward each other and build a strong
connection isn't just about feelings or enjoying each other.
It's a spiritual battle. There is a spirit of fear and a spirit of
love. Who you choose to partner with will carry over into the
environment around you. If you partner with fear and that is
your mentor, then you create a culture of fear around you, and
you will have relationships that are distant and disconnected.
You might end up thinking you just don't like people. Really,
it's the anxiety you're hosting that is creating that environment
around you.

Likewise, when you choose love, and a partnership with the
Spirit of love, you can believe in people you don't even know.
You can cheer people on who were at one point your enemy.
What gives you that courage? It is the eternal part of life, of
building a family, a home, of choosing to partner with the
Spirit of love.

*Father God, we want to partner with You—the Spirit of love.
We want to be the kind of people who believe in others and
encourage them in their faith regardless of how they make us
feel. Help us to have Your heart for people and show us how
to live by Your power.*

Which kingdom are you partnering with today?

RECRUITING DESTRUCTION

When I am afraid,
I will put my trust in you.
I praise God for what he has promised.
I trust in God, so why should I be afraid?
What can mere mortals do to me?

PSALM 56:3-4 NLT

It's important that you understand fear. It has a life and a real goal, and that goal is to kill, steal, and destroy. The essence of fear is to take away from your life. When you listen to and trust the spirit of fear, you have recruited destruction—into your marriage and into your family.

If you have a relational breakdown with your spouse, it might scare you. The lens you put on says, "I can control you. I will control you." This is the seduction of that spirit, that through intimidation and the threat of punishment, you can control other people. Instead of bringing you together, fear of disconnection drives you apart. If you were trained since you were young that you are powerless because someone else can control you, and you continue to believe that lie, you also think you can control other people. Don't align yourself with fear. Turn your love on.

God, when we are afraid, we will put our trust in You. You are light and love. Give us Your perspective so we can align ourselves with love and against fear.

Do you see areas where you have allowed fear to influence your behavior?

THE CHOICE

The LORD God took the man and put him in the Garden of Eden to cultivate it and tend it. The LORD God commanded the man, saying, "From any tree of the garden you may freely eat; but from the tree of the knowledge of good and evil you shall not eat, for on the day that you eat from it you will certainly die."

GENESIS 2:15-17 NASB

Kids are often schooled to believe they can be controlled. They feel like their life isn't something they have a real choice in, so there is nothing they can do about what they do or don't like. The greatest gift you can give to a child is not to control them but to teach them to control themselves. Children should feel powerful and respected even though they are small.

God Himself so values our freedom that in a perfect environment He gave mankind a choice to disobey, to rebel, and to walk away from Him. He created eternal paradise and gave us the option to choose somebody besides Him. What made the Garden of Eden perfect was that there was a choice. Understanding that God has great value for freedom, and that He created you to live in it, should change your paradigm for your relationship with your spouse. You have to realize that there is a line—a line where your life stops, and your spouse's life starts.

Creator God, thank You for the freedom of choice. You give us everything we need to thrive, and though we still choose ourselves, You continue to love and pursue us. Thank You.

Can you acknowledge God's value for freedom?

LIMITED CONTROL

"Do not judge, and you will not be judged. Do not condemn, and you will not be condemned. Forgive, and you will be forgiven."

LUKE 6:37 NIV

Where your life stops and your spouse's life starts is the point where your control is limited. It doesn't matter if you love them like crazy, you cannot control them. The only thing keeping you together is your connection. You really have no influence on how your spouse does what they do with their life outside of your connection.

Your relationship with the Lord has the same dynamic. He doesn't have control over you. He doesn't want it. He never has. He has always wanted you to be free. He chooses you. He owns His half of the relationship. What will you do? You are powerful. You can protect your connection to God and to your spouse by managing yourself. You manage you, and you have done all that you can to set yourself up for connection.

God, it's so hard not to judge others or want to control them. Help us to realize that we need only to manage ourselves, that the way in which we judge, we will also be judged. With that in mind, help us to have incredible grace for each other. May we give each other the freedom to choose as You have given us.

How does it feel to have limited control in your relationship?

THE BIGGEST PROBLEM

Let no debt remain outstanding, except the continuing debt to love one another, for whoever loves others has fulfilled the law.

ROMANS 13:8 NIV

Connection drives fear away. Losing connection invites that powerful, destructive force to come back. Once you realize you have a disconnection, you need to understand that is your biggest problem. If you don't solve that problem, all the other issues will not go away.

When you increase the love and protect your connection, fear is reduced. Do your part in lowering anxiety by laying off the control, punishment, and intimidation, and start sending messages of love. Then the defenses can come down and you can begin to reconnect. Make necessary adjustments to create a culture of connectedness, and instead of just surviving, you will both begin to thrive.

Father, show us where we have lost our connection. Show us where we have allowed fear to creep in. We want to lower anxiety and create an environment of closeness.

What messages of love can you send to your spouse today?

SWITCHED

"I give you now a new commandment:
Love each other just as much as I have loved you."
JOHN 13:34 TPT

In a marriage relationship, it's great when both switches are on, but there will always be times when one switch is on, and the other is off. When one spouse decides to keep their love off for whatever reason, it requires a lot of patience from the other spouse. The important thing to do is to keep your love on, and communicate things about yourself, not about them.

Tell your spouse how your lack of connection is affecting your heart and your relational experience without blaming or trying to control them. This level of vulnerability may be new to your relationship, but your spouse will respond differently to your hurt than they will to your angry judgment. The culture you begin to create will help change the dynamic and hopefully steer you back together more quickly.

God, Your unconditional love is both mind-blowing and sobering. It is always switched on. Thank You for Your patience that allows us to draw near without fear. Help us to be gentle with each other in the ways we communicate and to share the kind of love You have with us.

What can you do to change the dynamic in your relationship when you feel disconnected?

I'LL BE BACK

Walk in love, as Christ loved us and gave himself up for us,
a fragrant offering and sacrifice to God.
EPHESIANS 5:2 ESV

In a long-term relationship, sometimes the individual desire for connection may vary. When the motivation level for connection is different, what do you do? Marriage is a covenant relationship. You have to decide to keep your love on and choose connection. You may experience nuances in your connection, where you have interrupted connection for a time, but that isn't the problem. The bigger question is, how connected do you live?

If your spouse says their goal is distance, it's painful, but at least you know what you are dealing with. If your goal is connection, then you take an "I'll be back" mindset. You keep inviting heaven in and letting the love of God flow through your life. You don't control your spouse, but you do everything you know to lower the anxiety between you so it is easier for them to step back in, and you continue to hope they will.

God, there are so many times You could have given up on us and walked away. We are so fickle in our pursuit of You. We have a hard time staying connected to anyone because of our insecurities and weakness. Give us the staying power we need to love through times of disconnection.

How connected do you and your spouse live?

ENCOURAGING POWERFULNESS

Strengthen the hands that are weak and the knees that are feeble, and make straight paths for your feet, so that the limb which is impaired may not be dislocated, but rather be healed.

HEBREWS 12:12-13 NASB

Advising a powerless person to become powerful is challenging. They need to overcome a victim mentality. They really believe that something out there is more powerful than they are, so it feels like truth to blame their situations on something else. Whatever they believe to be true is true to them.

Their first step is to confront the lie that they are powerless and can't control themselves. If they were trained to be powerless in childhood, they may need to spend some time with a counselor or someone who can help them realize they are powerful. The motivation is not to control or change their spouse, but to be powerful over themselves. Sometimes it's just sitting with a counselor and looking at their spiritual beliefs and identity. If they don't learn a new set of skills, they will keep falling in the same ditch.

Jesus, You are truth. Speak truth to the lies we have believed and cause us to be strengthened with Your power. You can heal our past hurts and piece us back together. We are broken, but You are whole. Do the work in us that needs to be done so we can become powerful individually and together.

Is there someone you can talk to about becoming powerful?

NO JOKE

Let us therefore make every effort to do what leads to peace
and to mutual edification.

ROMANS 14:19 NIV

Your first years of marriage may have been great, or they
may have been a constant struggle. Serious challenges can
be created by vastly different personalities, broken relational
histories, and natural human fears. There either have been or
there will be plenty of moments where you could decide you've
had enough because it just isn't working.

The better choice is to stay invested in your connection
and keep trying. Choose to embrace the unique things that
make you different and learn what unconditional love and
acceptance can produce when two people refuse to give up on
each other.

*God, being married is hard work. Help us to continue to choose
each other and press forward in our relationship. We want to
stick together and encourage peace in our home, especially when
we feel like giving up. Thank You that You never give up on us.
We can learn so much from Your example.*

In moments you feel like giving up, how do you choose love?

FOUNTAIN OF HOPE

> May God, the fountain of hope, fill you to overflowing with
> uncontainable joy and perfect peace as you trust in him. And
> may the power of the Holy Spirit continually surround your
> life with his super-abundance until you radiate with hope!
>
> ROMANS 15:13 TPT

If you were blessed to grow up in a healthy relational
environment, then it is possible for you to simply inherit good
relational tools, never really appreciating just how powerful
and costly they are. But when you have to pay the price to go
find these tools after receiving a pile of dangerous, broken
tools from your family environment, then you have a different
perspective.

You need to acquire the tools and wisdom to build a healthy
connection in your marriage. Make the reversals from
powerless to powerful, from control to self-control, from
the goal of distance to the goal of connection, and from
fear to love. It may be nothing short of revolutionary. But
there is hope that you can build or restore healthy intimate
connections in your life even after years of disconnection and
brokenness.

*Holy Spirit, give us wisdom in assessing our relational tools. We
want to use good tools and throw away those that are broken,
useless, or harmful. Lead us in Your hope and fill us with joy as
we look to You to be our guide.*

How can you drink from the fountain of hope today?

BUILDING ON SAND

"Everyone who hears these words of mine and does not put them into practice is like a foolish man who built his house on sand."

MATTHEW 7:26 NIV

Healthy relationships truly are the most valuable, meaningful, and satisfying of human experiences. What are the qualities that make up a healthy relational connection? If you don't know, then you won't be able to assess whether or not your relational practices are helping to build and strengthen a connection.

Like a house, a relational connection needs to have specific elements to complete its structure, or it will be unsafe and vulnerable to disaster. Reading God's Word, and putting it into practice, will help you make sure you aren't building your relationship on sand.

Jesus, we know what You said about building on sand. Is that what we have done? Help us to put Your truth into practice and to build our relationship on You—the surest foundation there is. We want our structure to be safe and sound, ready to meet the storms of life and stay standing through them.

How might you be building your relationship on sand?

ONE FOUNDATION

No one can lay any foundation other than the one we already
have—Jesus Christ.
Anyone who builds on that foundation may use a variety of
materials—gold, silver, jewels, wood, hay, or straw. But on the
judgment day, fire will reveal what kind of work each builder
has done. The fire will show if a person's work has any value.

1 CORINTHIANS 3:11-13 NLT

As with all houses, building starts with the foundation.
The foundation of a healthy relationship is an agreement to
practice unconditional acceptance and unconditional love.
Unconditional acceptance says, "You are not me and I am not
you. You get to be you, and I get to be me in this relationship."
This does not mean you have to unconditionally accept one
another's behaviors. Rather, it means that you do not control
one another.

Build your relationship on the foundation of Christ using work
that is valuable, work that will not be burned by fire, work that
will last.

*God, what kind of work are we building here? Help us to be
honest in our assessment of our relationship. We want to build
on You and with You, not looking to control each other, but to
serve and give. Let our work be that which will not be burned up
in the fire.*

What foundation is your relationship built on?

PROTECTED CONNECTION

Let the morning bring me word of your unfailing love,
for I have put my trust in you.
Show me the way I should go,
for to you I entrust my life.

PSALM 143:8 NIV

People can't force their way into your home, or into your trust, vulnerability, or intimacy. You are the only person who allows people into your house. This does not mean you are controlling other people; rather, you are controlling yourself.

Unconditional love says to your spouse that no matter what they do, you will continue to pursue the goal of connection with them. Anxiety naturally arises when personal differences show up in your relationship, and fear will tempt you to run away from each other. But in committing to unconditional love, you commit to keep moving toward each other even when you are scared. You do whatever you need to do to protect your connection.

God, thank You for Your love that is unfailing, unlimited, and trustworthy. Help us in our attempts to love each other unconditionally. We want to move together, not apart. Show us how to do that in a way that isn't controlling.

How do you protect your connection?

No Wedges

> "If a kingdom is divided against itself, that kingdom cannot stand. And if a house is divided against itself, that house will not be able to stand."
>
> MARK 3:24-25 ESV

Sometimes you have to be willing to agree to disagree over something in order to maintain your connection. Relationships can almost be destroyed over different opinions on certain issues, especially if you have intense conversations around those issues. If you try to control each other by getting the other person to agree with you, it can create a large divide.

When you decide to put your relationship first and be at peace even though you approach an issue differently, you can continue to be in relationship together. You may never agree on certain things, but you don't let that disagreement create a wedge in your connection.

God, You dwell in perfect unity with Your Son and the Holy Spirit. Thank You that Your kingdom is not divided against itself. Please show us how to have grace-filled conversations when differences are present. We don't want to allow wedges in our connection.

Is there something you need to agree to disagree about in order to preserve your relationship?

CONDITIONAL

You gave me life and showed me your unfailing love.
My life was preserved by your care.

JOB 10:12 NLT

Conditional love and acceptance mean that you are willing to pull away from your connection under certain circumstances. The minute you scare your spouse, or they scare you, you will be tempted to withhold your love and disconnect.

Because disconnection only produces more fear and anxiety, you will widen your distance at an alarming rate. This threat effectively prevents the two of you from feeling free to be yourselves because you instinctively know the connection won't be strong enough to handle it. Unconditional love and care will help preserve your relationship and strengthen your connection.

Father, thank You for loving us just the way we are. Show us how to better love and care for one another, so we can stay tightly connected and live together without fear. Help us to be vulnerable enough to be ourselves.

Do you both feel free to be yourselves around each other?

SLAVE TO NOTHING

"I am allowed to do anything"—but not everything is good for
you. And even though "I am allowed to do anything," I must
not become a slave to anything.

1 CORINTHIANS 6:12 NLT

When you commit to unconditional love and acceptance, you
protect each other's freedom. Everything that you offer to the
relationship comes freely from your heart, not under coercion.

Committing to pursue and protect your connection with
each other means that you are both thinking about how your
decisions will affect the other person and making adjustments
accordingly. Managing yourselves to protect your connection
is the ultimate expression of freedom, and that is what it means
to be a powerful person.

*God, You have given us so much freedom through Your
unconditional love that we don't have to be slaves to anything.
We want to protect that freedom and strengthen our connection
by managing ourselves and not trying to control each other. Help
us to be mindful of each other as we make decisions that will
affect our relationship.*

*What adjustments do you need to make
in order to positively affect your spouse?*

GUARANTEED CHOICE

Our great desire is that you will keep on loving others as long
as life lasts, in order to make certain that what you hope for
will come true.

HEBREWS 6:11 NLT

Without the foundation of unconditional love and acceptance
in a relationship, you simply cannot be free to be yourself.
It's only when you remove the option of distance and
disconnection from your relationship that you create a safe
place to be yourself. You cast out fear, inviting each other to
bring your best selves forward.

Yes, it's vulnerable and scary to keep your love on toward
someone who has become a perceived threat; you cannot
guarantee what they are going to do. But you can guarantee
your own choice. And you can always choose connection.

*Father, You love us even when we are broken and ugly. Thank
You for picking up the pieces and creating a safe place for our
hope to be renewed. Because of Your love for us, we can have a
similar love for each other. We choose connection again today.*

How can you choose connection with your spouse today?

SEVEN PILLARS

Wisdom has built her house,
She has carved out her seven pillars.
PROVERBS 9:1 NASB

The foundation of unconditional love and acceptance determines the longevity and resilience of a relational connection. This foundation consistently supports the other elements that make up a healthy relationship.

The house of Wisdom represents the Kingdom of God, the domain where God's ultimate reality is expressed in its perfect design. At the center of this kingdom is the dynamic and perfect relationship of the Trinity, which sets the pattern for all relationships. The pillars that hold up this house represent the core values of healthy relationships. These core values are love, honor, self-control, responsibility, truth, faith, and vision.

God, we want to dwell in Your house of wisdom. You are perfect, and You see everything with the right perspective and heart. We want the core values of love, honor, self-control, responsibility, truth, faith, and vision to be evident in our relationship. Keep us under Your instruction so we can see how to do that.

How do you see the seven pillars representing the core values of healthy relationships?

PILLAR OF LOVE

Now faith, hope, and love abide, these three;
but the greatest of these is love.
1 CORINTHIANS 13:13 ESV

Love is a word of many meanings. It is used to talk about favorite sports, foods, hobbies, and movies. We also read and acknowledge in the Scripture above, that love is the biggest, most important, and most powerful thing in the universe. But what does love mean in the context of a relationship?

The pillar of love is comprised of a commitment, an action, and a result. The commitment part says you care about and value your spouse—all of them. You care about their soul, spirit, body, relationships, dreams, and destiny. The action part is demonstrating care and value in many ways and situations as you get to know them over time. And the result of these actions is that your spouse feels loved! They feel safe, valued, connected, nourished, protected, and understood.

God, help us to establish a strong pillar of love in our relationship. We want each other to feel loved and cared about. Help us to show love in a way that our spouse receives it.

How is the pillar of love standing in your relationship?

LOVE PRODUCT

The goal of this command is love, which comes from a pure heart and a good conscience and a sincere faith.

1 TIMOTHY 1:5 NIV

If your love isn't producing things like safety, peace, and trust in your relationship, it probably shouldn't be called love. There are millions of people around the world who call what they have in a relationship "love." Looking closer, you find that they are people who cannot fully be themselves because it's not safe.

If you want to test the quality of love in a relationship, then you need to ask one another, "Do you feel safe? Do you feel cared for? Do you feel valued and significant? Do you feel protected? Do you feel pursued and known?" Remember, perfect love casts out fear. The most immediate sign that the pillar of love is growing strong in your relationship is that all fear is leaving as courage, freedom, and safety are felt and expressed.

God, we want the pillar of love to be strong in our marriage. Remind us that it is in and through Your love for us that we can increase the quality of our love for each other. Help us to create a safe environment for our love to grow.

Is the pillar of love successfully removing fear from your relationship?

WHAT LOVE IS

Love is patient and kind. Love is not jealous or boastful or proud or rude. It does not demand its own way. It is not irritable, and it keeps no record of being wronged. It does not rejoice about injustice but rejoices whenever the truth wins out. Love never gives up, never loses faith, is always hopeful, and endures through every circumstance.

1 CORINTHIANS 13:4-7 NLT

The construct of the relationship pillars starts with love. The reason love is the foundation is that love is learning how to create a safe place. If you are not experiencing safety and connection with each other, and you say you love each other, then it's difficult to know what love really means. If love isn't safety and connection, then it's probably something no one wants.

When you establish the pillar of love, it is a safe place to be vulnerable. You can show each other your hearts and you know you are both moving toward each other. When you say, "I love you," it means that you have created a safe place for you and your spouse to connect.

Father God, help us to provide a space place of love where we can dwell together. You are the truest example of love, and we want to be like You. Give us strength to continue moving toward deeper connection with You and with each other.

What does love mean to you?

PILLAR OF HONOR

Whoever pursues righteousness and unfailing love
will find life, righteousness, and honor.

PROVERBS 21:21 NLT

Honor, like submission, is a term that has been misused and
abused, particularly in connection with marriage. People see
it as something that is expected, rather than something that is
given. This is backwards.

When honor is expected or even demanded, it becomes just
another word for handing the control, power, and value over
to one person in the relationship. A relationship where one
person has all the power is one of dishonor, not honor. Honor
means showing respect for someone you believe holds great
worth. You show honor; you don't demand it.

*God, You deserve all of our honor and praise. We submit to You
because You are perfect and holy. Your kindness has drawn us
into deeper connection with You. Show us how to give honor and
respect that comes from a place of value and worth.*

How is the pillar of honor standing in your relationship?

PATTERN FOR HONOR

Now we're no longer living like slaves under the law,
but we enjoy being God's very own sons and daughters!
And because we're his, we can access everything our Father
has—for we are heirs because of what God has done!

GALATIANS 4:7 TPT

God modeled honor when He transformed us from slaves to friends, from orphans to children. He stooped low to bring us to His level. He used His power to make us powerful, insisting that we be equal partners in His plan to bring heaven to earth. This is the pattern for honor in relationships.

True honor is the practice of two powerful people putting one another before themselves, empowering one another, working together to meet each other's needs, and adjusting as necessary in order to move together toward the shared goals of the relationship. Honor is also the practice of calling out the best in one another.

Father, help us to build a pillar of honor that creates an environment where we put others above ourselves. We want to work together to make our goal of connection a reality, encouraging each other by calling out the best in each of us.

How do you honor and empower each other?

HONORING DIFFERENCES

Recognize the value of every person and continually show love to every believer. Live your lives with great reverence and in holy awe of God.

1 PETER 2:17 TPT

Honor allows you to keep high levels of value for and faith in people, even when they demonstrate how different from you they are (which can be scary) and when they make mistakes (which can also be scary).

Typically, people allow differences and mistakes to lower their respect and value for other people. But you know the pillar of honor is strong in a relationship when you can look at your spouse and say, "You are really different from me. It makes me sad when I see you making that choice. But I love you. I value you, I believe in you, and I am here for you in this relationship."

God, help us to honor and value each other even through our differences. We want to have grace for each other, knowing we will continue to make mistakes, but we are committed to our marriage and to loving well.

Can you keep your level of value high even when differences and mistakes are present?

OF VALUE

Wisdom's instruction is to fear the LORD,
and humility comes before honor.
PROVERBS 15:33 NIV

Honor is the experience created by two powerful people. It doesn't work if you and your spouse are taking turns being powerful. You both live powerfully and understand that what you have brought to the table as individuals is valuable. What you each think, say, and need remains powerful even when you disagree.

Honor preserves the two of you powerful people working together to meet the needs of each other in every situation.

God, You have created us as equals. We are both valuable to You, and what we think, feel, and say matters. Help us to honor each other, demonstrating humility and remaining powerful as individuals.

How do you ensure your spouse feels valuable?

PILLAR OF SELF-CONTROL

The end of all things is at hand; therefore be self-controlled
and sober-minded for the sake of your prayers.

1 PETER 4:7 ESV

Self-control is at the core of being a powerful person. Self-
control means that you can tell yourself what to do, and you
can make yourself do it. It sounds simple enough, but telling
yourself what to do and obeying yourself can be quite an
accomplishment! For most, it's a good day when they obey
themselves.

To practice self-control, you must have a goal. You must have
something you are saying yes to, which necessarily comes
with things that you must say no to. You use self-control to
maneuver yourself toward the yes. This goal must be entirely
your own. The minute another person is choosing and
managing your goals for you, you have left self-control behind.

*God, help us to be self-controlled and alert. We want to be able
to say yes to things that build closeness and no to those things
that don't. Give us wisdom to know the difference.*

How is the pillar of self-control standing in your relationship?

FOLLOW THROUGH

> Above all we must be those who never need to verify our speech as truthful by swearing by the heavens or the earth or any other oath. But instead we must be so full of integrity that our "Yes" or "No" is convincing enough and we do not stumble into hypocrisy.
>
> JAMES 5:12 TPT

When you practice self-control in a relationship, you take full responsibility for managing your love and pursuing your goal of connection. If you ever turn your love off toward your spouse, it is 100% your fault, no matter what they may have done. Self-control removes the option of blaming others for your choices.

When two people show one another they are able to control themselves on a consistent basis, they demonstrate they are reliable and trustworthy. You can tell the pillar of self-control is strong in a relationship when you don't have to spend time wondering whether or not the other person will follow through with something they promised to do.

God, we want to be dependable. We want our word to count for something. Help us to be able to rely on each other when it matters the most.

Can you rely on each other to follow through on your promises?

MANAGING FREEDOM

Now you are free from the power of sin and have become
slaves of God. Now you do those things that lead to holiness
and result in eternal life.

ROMANS 6:22 NLT

Self-control is at the core of being a powerful person. Conversely,
a lack of self-control creates anxiety in a relationship because
you cannot trust one another to manage yourselves toward your
goals. You may be trusted to manage your own time at a job, for
example. Your boss doesn't feel the need to hover over you. But
if you happen to become involved in a relationship shortly after
getting that job and you begin to replace your priority of work
with priority of relationship, your work might pile up, stressing
out you, your boss, and everyone else who depends on you to do
what you said you would do. The end result is a jeopardized job
and relationship with your boss.

You must learn how to manage your freedom. When you have
more freedom than self-control, then that freedom erodes the
quality of your life and friendships. Self-control is what allows
you to manage increasing levels of freedom in your life and
relationships.

*Father, thank You for the freedom You have given us. We want
to manage our freedom with integrity and a choice for our
marriage.*

*How do you use self-control to manage the freedoms
in your life and relationship?*

CHAMPION ATHLETES

A true athlete will be disciplined in every respect, practicing constant self-control in order to win a laurel wreath that quickly withers. But we run our race to win a victor's crown that will last forever. For that reason, I don't run just for exercise or box like one throwing aimless punches, but I train like a champion athlete. I subdue my body and get it under my control, so that after preaching the good news to others I myself won't be disqualified.

1 CORINTHIANS 9:25-27 TPT

The pillar of self-control is the agreement that it's not your job to control your spouse, nor is it theirs to control you. You each have the job of controlling yourselves only. This allows you to hold one another accountable, to communicate, and to live responsibly.

When self-control is strong for both of you, then you don't fall into the practice or habit of controlling each other even if that is what you would like to do sometimes. If you don't control yourself, you are out of control. The same goes for your spouse. Make self-control a characteristic of your relationship.

Jesus, You practiced self-control in the most inspiring way when You walked the earth. Help us to train like champion athletes, bringing our bodies and minds under control, so we are better able to serve You and each other.

How disciplined are you?

PILLAR OF RESPONSIBILITY

You, then, why do you judge your brother or sister?
Or why do you treat them with contempt?
For we will all stand before God's judgment seat. It is written:
"'As surely as I live,' says the Lord,
'every knee will bow before me;
every tongue will acknowledge God.'"
So then, each of us will give an account of ourselves to God.

ROMANS 14:10-12 NIV

If you break down the word *responsibility*, it literally means "ability to respond." A response is the opposite of a reaction. "Response-ability" is the capacity to face any situation and make powerful choices that are consistent with who you say you are.

You refuse to run away from difficulties or any part of your life or reality that you happen to dislike. When you take full ownership of your life in this way, you gain confidence and momentum in making good decisions.

God, thank You for the ability to respond in a manner that is pleasing to You and demonstrates love for each other. You are our confidence and strength. Our ability to make good decisions and take responsibility for our actions lies in our close connection with You.

How is the pillar of responsibility standing in your relationship?

ON HIGH ALERT

Seek his will in all you do,
and he will show you which path to take.
PROVERBS 3:6 NLT

If you spent a day driving around New York City without a map, your anxiety levels would likely be elevated into what could be called crisis territory. At each intersection you'd crane your neck to read the street signs, with senses on high alert in the swirl of honking taxis and pedestrians. Every hundred feet or so, you'd have to make another decision about where to go, which would become more and more difficult as you realized you had no idea where you were. Responding to this kind of environment is difficult to say the least.

But if you head to New York with a GPS that tells you where to turn and how far away your destination is, your anxiety stays low because you trust that your GPS is going to lead you down the right path. If you make a mistake, you can count on it to show you a different route. You are able to respond to your circumstances and get where you want to go. In your relationship with your spouse, you can count on God to guide you on the path toward better connectedness and choosing love.

Father, You are the one we look to for guidance. Help us to be sensitive to Your instruction as we seek Your will together.

How has God guided you in your relationship?

CONFIDENT CHOICE

As for us, we have all of these great witnesses who encircle us like clouds. So we must let go of every wound that has pierced us and the sin we so easily fall into. Then we will be able to run life's marathon race with passion and determination, for the path has been already marked out before us.

We look away from the natural realm and we focus our attention and expectation onto Jesus who birthed faith within us and who leads us forward into faith's perfection.

HEBREWS 12:1-2 TPT

When the pillar of responsibility is strong in a relationship, it's like having a GPS. Both you and your spouse are confident and relaxed because you have a plan, an inner compass, that can be relied on to help you respond with love and make good, powerful choices in any circumstance.

This plan grows out of your core commitments to control yourselves, cast out fear with love, and pursue the goal of connection. It's very powerful when the two of you can look at one another and know that no matter what happens, you know what both of you are going to choose to do.

God, we want to continue to choose love—for You and for each other. Show us how to run with enduring passion and determination. We fix our eyes on You again today.

Are you confident in your spouse's responses?

NOT WANDERING

How can a young man keep his way pure?
By guarding it according to your word.
With my whole heart I seek you;
let me not wander from your commandments!

PSALM 119:9-10 ESV

When you demonstrate an ability to respond, you have a plan. You know what you are going to do when something happens. If you don't know where you are headed, you won't have any idea which way you should go to arrive at destination Nowhere. You'll be swept up by whatever catches your eye, wasting precious time and resources. This is what you'd call reacting to life.

If you have something or somewhere specific you are working toward, and you are managing yourself in it, then you have a plan, and you will know how to respond to different situations. If you and your spouse disconnect, you are able to respond because you have a plan to move toward them, to keep your love on, and to communicate that you care about your marriage relationship and connection.

God, we don't want to wander aimlessly. Help us to seek You with our whole hearts, and to remember that our plan is always to move toward each other.

How can you keep yourself from wandering?

QUALITY OF TRUST

Trust in the LORD forever,
For in GOD the LORD, we have an everlasting Rock.

ISAIAH 26:4 NASB

If you were asked to write down a list of qualities you wanted in your relationship, trust or trustworthiness would likely be somewhere close to the top. But, if trust means you need to be able to anticipate your spouse's decisions and know that they would do what you would do, your connection can be easily threatened.

On one level, it's right that two people in a relationship need to be on the same page about who they are and what they are going after. But if trust hinges on your ability to anticipate your spouse's behavior, you lose trust every time they do something you would never do. This version of trust quickly turns to mistrust, which is just another word for fear—the enemy of love and connection.

God, You are the only one who is completely trustworthy. Help us to have grace for each other in our weakness and failure. You are our rock, and we trust You with everything we have and everything we need.

Does the quality of trust rank high on your list?
Do you see where it could be problematic?

PILLAR OF TRUTH

Let us not love in word or talk but in deed and in truth.
By this we shall know that we are of the truth and reassure our
heart before him; for whenever our heart condemns us, God is
greater than our heart, and he knows everything.

1 JOHN 3:18-20 ESV

Many people get disillusioned and hurt when God does not
do what they think He should have done. Because they could
not predict His behavior, they decide not to trust Him. Does
that mean God is not trustworthy? Absolutely not. If God who
is perfect is not trustworthy, then how can imperfect people
ever be trustworthy? You need to be able to trust people even
when they do things you wouldn't do, or you will end up very
isolated.

Two people who walk through life together are always getting
to know one another on some level. Life is not static or
contained. There will be mystery, unexpected circumstances,
and fresh seasons of growth. There is a pillar that makes room
for this—the pillar of truth. The pillar of truth sustains trust in
a relationship. You display trust by telling the truth.

Holy Spirit, help us to live before one another in truth. Even
when it is difficult to be honest, we pray that You would help
that to be our choice. We want the pillar of truth to be strong in
our relationship.

How is the pillar of truth standing in your relationship?

GOOD INFORMATION

Teach me Your way, O LORD;
I will walk in Your truth;
Unite my heart to fear Your name.
PSALM 86:11 NKJV

Like all the other pillars, truth is built through powerful choices, choices that are all about what you are going to do, not about what your spouse is going to do. You don't demand their trust; you display trust by telling the truth. You give your spouse the opportunity to see what is going on inside of you. Choose to show each other what you are experiencing in your marriage relationship, no matter what.

When you and your spouse practice this, you leave each other with good information, and you get to make better decisions because you begin to see each other more clearly. Practicing truth is vulnerable but absolutely necessary when building any relationship worth keeping.

Father, sometimes practicing truth hurts. We know that the benefit is well worth it, so help us to be vulnerable enough to let each other in. Teach us how to be loving, gracious, and kind so vulnerability becomes natural between us.

How do you practice truth with each other?

MANAGING TRUST

He was despised and rejected—
a man of sorrows, acquainted with deepest grief.
We turned our backs on him and looked the other way.
He was despised, and we did not care.

ISAIAH 53:3 NLT

Once one of you has opened up and been vulnerable, the other has a choice to make. Will you meet halfway and exchange more truth? That would be optimal. But even if it doesn't happen that way, you each still control your own truth. You continue to show your truth and demonstrate trust regardless of your spouse's actions.

Jesus managed His trust in ways that would scare the pants off most people. Think about this—on the night His disciples would betray and abandon Him, He brought them around the table and said, "Let's make a covenant." What kind of person says, "Hey you betrayers, come get closer, let me deepen my covenant with you right before you break yours with Me"? Someone who really knows how to manage His trust—that's who! Jesus' trust wasn't dependent on you, and your trust shouldn't be dependent on your spouse.

Jesus, thank You for showing truth and demonstrating trust even when You knew You would be betrayed. We want to learn from Your example and have the same mind. Let our trust be dependent on You and not each other.

How can you ensure your trust isn't dependent on your spouse?

DEEPEST NEEDS

If you have been raised with Christ, keep seeking the things that are above, where Christ is, seated at the right hand of God. Set your minds on the things that are above, not on the things that are on earth.

COLOSSIANS 3:1-2 NASB

Many addiction recovery programs teach people they need to pursue a connection with God if they want to break out of bondage from a substance or activity. This aspect of recovery acknowledges that the other side of human instinct to avoid pain is the instinct to grab hold of things that calm anxiety and feel good—things that bring comfort, safety, and pleasure.

You both have a deep, God-created need for intimacy, love, and comfort. But if you look to things that were not designed to meet these needs and elevate them above everything else—making them idols—then the result is always bondage and destruction. It's only when you place God at the center that you can access the comfort, peace, safety, joy, and pleasure that truly meets your deepest needs. Only faith in the Creator can make you truly free.

God, we admit our need for You again today. There is nothing in this world that can satisfy us like You do. Be present with us today and fill us with Your joy, peace, and true freedom.

How can you make God the center of your relationship?

SET UP

Don't set the affections of your heart on this world or in loving the things of the world. The love of the Father and the love of the world are incompatible. For all that the world can offer us—the gratification of our flesh, the allurement of the things of the world, and the obsession with status and importance— none of these things come from the Father but from the world. This world and its desires are in the process of passing away, but those who love to do the will of God live forever.

1 JOHN 2:15-17 TPT

When you put your spouse in the position of God, you set them up for failure. If you think your spouse is responsible for your joy, identity, and comfort—all things that only God should satisfy—you will be sorely disappointed. Inevitably, your anxiety will go through the roof whenever you can't control your spouse.

Putting your spouse in charge of meeting your deepest needs creates a situation where you become afraid of them. They are your addiction, and when you can't get your fix, you end up in a horrible mess. Your only hope is to turn to God. He must be the one who satisfies your needs. No one else can handle this "God job" like He can.

God, we give You the rightful position of provider and protector in our lives. You will meet our deepest needs, and we ask You to do that today. We place our hope fully in You.

Have you given your spouse God's job?
How can you give it back to God?

SUPREME ACCOUNTABILITY

The word of God is living and active, sharper than any two-edged sword, piercing to the division of soul and of spirit, of joints and of marrow, and discerning the thoughts and intentions of the heart. And no creature is hidden from his sight, but all are naked and exposed to the eyes of him to whom we must give account.

HEBREWS 4:12-13 ESV

Mysterious as it is, making yourself accountable to God and putting yourself under His authority is the only way you can become powerful and learn to govern yourself. The founding fathers of the United States understood this very well. They taught that a free society is only free when individuals submit themselves by faith to divine authority and a code of virtue. The moment you remove faith from a society, you remove the possibility of self-government.

If you choose not to be accountable to God, you cannot be relied on to govern yourself. Encourage each other today to live according to His Word and walk together in the grace He has so mercifully provided.

Jesus, You are the living Word of God. We ask You to help us walk with accountability to You and other trusted believers in our lives. Teach us how to live in submission to Your divine authority.

What do you do to live in accountability to God?

EXCHANGE OF TRUTH

Those who know your name trust in you,
for you, LORD, have never forsaken those who seek you.
PSALM 9:10 NIV

What builds trust in a relationship is the exchange of truth.
Truth isn't just what you think about each other, your polished
judgments, or your scriptural corrections for one another.
Truth isn't what comes from one person to the other. Truth is
the revelation of what's going on inside of each person.

When you exchange truth with your spouse, you show them
what's inside of you. Then they have much better information.
It gives you both the opportunity to create and grow your
intimacy. It can be scary to offer truth when there isn't
unconditional love as a foundation in your relationship, but in
order to experience real trust in a relationship, you have to be
able to exchange truth.

*God, You are so trustworthy. Thank You that no matter what
truth we share about ourselves with You, You meet us with
unconditional love and acceptance. Help us to show the same
to each other in our moments of vulnerability.*

Have you exchanged truth with each other lately?

PILLAR OF FAITH

We have known and believed the love that God has for us. God is love, and he who abides in love abides in God, and God in him.

1 JOHN 4:16 NKJV

The pillar of faith is built in a relationship as you commit to keep God as your ultimate source, ultimate comforter, and ultimate authority. The result of this commitment is that both of you are able to govern yourselves and access a boundless well of spiritual resources that will sustain you in moving toward your relational goals.

When you both consistently pursue a connection with the Perfect One, that connection will set the pace for your connection with each other. You will find increased wisdom, strength, peace, hope, joy, and more. But most of all, you will learn to love from Love Himself, which can only bring the best into your relationship.

Perfect One, thank You for the love we find in You. As we abide with You, You will show us how to love as You love. We want to be deeply connected with You so our connection with each other is strengthened as well.

How is the pillar of faith standing in your relationship?

TURN YOUR ATTENTION

Seek the LORD while you can find him.
Call on him now while he is near.
Let the wicked change their ways
and banish the very thought of doing wrong.
Let them turn to the LORD that he may have mercy on them.
Yes, turn to our God, for he will forgive generously.

ISAIAH 55:6-7 NLT

The pain and the fear that comes from being disconnected in a relationship usually leaves you feeling powerless to do anything about it. Unless you both turn your attention to God after an argument, you may feel controlled or despondent in your distance.

After you disconnect, you must turn your attention to God until you are able to connect. This is the only way to lessen anxiety, reestablish the goal of love, and gain a supernatural energy to reconnect.

God, how we need Your mercy and love. Every time we come to You in repentance, You forgive us and strengthen us. We want You to be the first place we turn when we are at odds with each other, so we can receive grace from You and then extend it to each other.

*How can you turn your attention to God
in difficult relational moments?*

END OF YOURSELF

"I tell you, you can pray for anything, and if you believe that
you've received it, it will be yours."

MARK 11:24 NLT

When you embrace the pillar of faith, you acknowledge that
you need help, much more help than you can provide for
yourselves. You need access to a supernatural God who can
bring resources, change, or revelation into your life when
you don't know what to do, or when you don't see something
coming.

At some point in your marriage, you will each come to the end
of yourselves and realize there is nothing more you can do.
Being in a committed relationship is hard work, and it is good
to put in every last bit of effort you have. But eventually, you will
have nothing left to give. And that is where you must have faith.
Faith is submitting and surrendering your relationship to God.

*God, we surrender ourselves and our relationship to You. You
know how to get us to where we need to be. You can show us
what we each need to do to make this relationship a joy and
blessing, not only to us but to those we are in community with.
We trust You with our marriage.*

Have you experienced the need for faith in your relationship?

PILLAR OF VISION

Be diligent in these matters; give yourself wholly to them,
so that everyone may see your progress.

1 TIMOTHY 4:15 NIV

One of the marks of powerful people is that they proactively establish practices and build relationships that help to renew their vision and remind them of who they are.

When you and your spouse establish the pillar of vision in your relationship, you share the knowledge of each other's identity and calling, as well as your joint vision, and you remind one another of these things on a regular basis. When seasons of difficulty, pain, or loss come up, the pillar of vision strengthens your relational connection and protects it from being thrown into survival mode.

God, help us to set up good practices that move us toward our shared vision. Give us the grace to accept and encourage our individual identities and callings as well. We want to be diligent in practicing that which is honoring to You.

How is the pillar of vision standing in your marriage?

IDENTITY AND CALLING

Be all the more diligent to make certain about His calling and choice of you; for as long as you practice these things, you will never stumble.

2 PETER 1:10 NASB

What is your identity and calling? What were you created to be and to do? The Holy Spirit is committed to helping you both find what that is, but you are responsible for making it happen. No one else can fulfill your potential.

You each have to embark on your own quest to discover why you are on this planet, what makes you get out of bed in the morning, and what you uniquely contribute to the world. Hopefully, you can both see gifts and passions in each other that you can affirm and encourage along the way.

God, we want to encourage each other on the journey of finding our identity and calling. Holy Spirit, show us what we were uniquely created to be and do. As we discover our purpose, help us to walk boldly into it, knowing You are fully with us and for us.

What do you think your purpose is?

SHARED VISION

May the God of endurance and encouragement grant you to
live in such harmony with one another, in accord with Christ
Jesus, that together you may with one voice glorify the God
and Father of our Lord Jesus Christ.

ROMANS 15:5-6 ESV

Along with a personal vision, you and your spouse need a
shared vision if you are going to have a healthy relationship.
Some couples have the vision to create the ideal Christian
marriage. Other couples want to create a 100-million-dollar
business together. Some want to serve as missionaries.

Whatever the goal, a shared vision is necessary in order to
move together in managing your priorities and preserving
unity. Moving independently toward your own visions will
not promote connectedness. It is important that you discover
together what your marriage goal is and move toward that goal
mutually.

*God, help us to discover our shared vision. Give us passion
and energy to move toward it together. We know it could mean
rearranging our priorities, but we want to be unified, so we ask
for the strength to do what we need to do.*

What is your shared vision?

PURPOSE TO ENDURE

Where there is no vision
the people are unrestrained.
PROVERBS 29:18 NASB

Some people never gain a vision for their identity and calling and stumble blindly and aimlessly through life, existing at the level of survival. Others do get a vision but lose sight of it through traumatic events or their own neglect.

One of the reasons you perish without a vision is that you cannot endure the pain and cost required to achieve any worthwhile purpose. Only vision can give a purpose to your pain, which enables you to endure it and reach your goal. Christ demonstrated this incredible power of vision when He went to the cross.

Jesus, thank You for Your sacrifice. Thank You for enduring the cross, showing us how important it is to have a clear vision for our identity and calling. Help us to have the endurance we need to continue in our shared vision for our marriage.

What might you have to endure to fulfill your shared vision?

THE FRONT PORCH

No wonder we don't give up.
For even though our outer person gradually wears out,
our inner being is renewed every single day.
2 CORINTHIANS 4:16 TPT

Your shared vision is that point in the distance that, as you move toward it, causes you to actually get closer together. Many people have a vision that's ten years out, like buying a house. But real vision stretches beyond that point to when you are 100 years old, sitting on your front porch, reminiscing about your life. What did you do with your love? How did you care for your family?

You and your spouse have a special vision because you are two unique people. What will you do with your lives? Imagine the front porch in sixty years. Assign that as the point of destiny. Don't sell yourselves short. Don't be those people who say they drifted apart. Keep your love on and build a life that keeps you engaged and excited.

God, thank You for making us special. We appreciate that our relationship dynamic is different than those around us. Give us the right kind of vision that leads us toward togetherness and two seats on the front porch in sixty years.

How do you picture growing old together?

ENVIRONMENT OF SHALOM

"My presence will go with you,
and I will give you rest."
EXODUS 33:14 ESV

When you and your spouse lay a firm foundation of unconditional love and acceptance and actively build the pillars of love, honor, self-control, responsibility, truth, faith, and vision in your connection, you raise a structure that can protect and cultivate an environment of shalom.

Shalom is a powerful Hebrew word that encompasses the flourishing of divine order, divine health, and divine prosperity in your life. It means that every part of your life—body, soul, spirit, relationships, dreams, and work—is being nourished and is growing and thriving. Shalom is the reality of God's kingdom of righteousness, peace, and joy being expressed in your life.

God of peace, we want to cultivate an environment of shalom. Help us to find the nourishment we need in You. Remind us that You are with us, and You give us rest. Thank You for Your Word that encourages growth and causes us to thrive in You.

How can you create an environment of shalom in your home?

ONLY YOU

My old self has been crucified with Christ.
It is no longer I who live, but Christ lives in me.
So I live in this earthly body by trusting in the Son of God,
who loved me and gave himself for me.
GALATIANS 2:20 NLT

Do you want the highest level of quality in your connection?
Do you want your relationship to invite shalom? Go after each
of the relational pillars! Examine your current thinking and
behavior in each area. Ask yourselves if others can truly be
themselves around you. Decide if you are moving toward each
other no matter what. Are you showing each other the truth of
your hearts? Do you respond well in situations, or do you react
and blame your choices on other people or things?

Nobody can manage your love but you. Nobody can manage
your honor or truth but you. Nobody can manage your self-
control or responsibility but you. And nobody can manage
your vision and your faith but you. The quality of what you are
building is ultimately up to you.

*God, help us to build these pillars of relationship on the
foundation of Your Son, Jesus. Thank You for giving us
everything we need to move toward each other in love.*

How good is the quality of the pillars you are building?

COVENANT KEEPER

"The mountains may move
and the hills disappear,
but even then my faithful love for you will remain.
My covenant of blessing will never be broken,"
Says the LORD, who has mercy on you.

ISAIAH 54:10 NLT

You and your spouse may have come from a family background that was less than ideal. Perhaps the standards of covenant, commitment, and keeping your love on were set very low. Maybe you have experienced a lot of broken relationships around you. It's possible that you hardly know anybody who has stayed married. These experiences affect your marriage expectations.

You might have been totally unprepared for marriage. If you and your spouse are completely different, you could even be considered incompatible. But you are married now! So, surround yourselves with other believers who are practicing true covenant and choose to keep your love on.

God, thank You so much for keeping Your covenant with us. Even though we are weak and flawed, You continue to love and bless us with Your mercy. Give us the staying power to stick to our covenant of love.

*What was your example of covenant growing up?
Do you see that affecting your expectations?*

SO DIFFERENT

"Why do you see the speck that is in your brother's eye,
but do not notice the log that is in your own eye?"
MATTHEW 7:3 ESV

Unconditional love means you get to be yourselves around
each other. It shouldn't be your mission in life to turn the other
person into you. You may have been attracted to each other
because you were so different, and at the beginning that was
exciting and perhaps even romantic.

Soon, you begin to view those differences as annoying,
frustrating, infuriating, or sometimes even wrong. Then you
start trying to change each other, to a point where you can't be
yourselves. You want your spouse to be like you. That would
make you both happy, right? Wrong. But there is hope. You can
still build a foundation of unconditional love. The seven pillars
of healthy relationships can get you there.

*Father, please help us. There are differences between us that
seem insurmountable at times. Give us Your perspective. Help
us to accept our differences and move toward unconditional love
for each other.*

How different are you and your spouse from each other?

TWO BECOME ONE

"'The two shall become one flesh';
so then they are no longer two, but one flesh."
MARK 10:8 NKJV

Some marriage vows date back to the Bible: "And the two shall become one." Doesn't that sound beautifully romantic? And then the couple spends the next twenty-five years fighting over which one they will become. There are two people in your relationship, and the job of covenant is to create a place where both of you can show up.

This doesn't mean you have to accept all behavior and not give any feedback on how it affects you, but it's not your job to change each other. It's your job to love each other. This foundation of unconditional love is what the pillars stand on. The pillars support a house that has peace, hope, and joy. It takes work to get there, but the pillars will build the life you want to live together.

Thank You, Father, that You joined us together as one flesh. Give us wisdom that allows for differences but gently challenges wrong living or thinking. Help us to love unconditionally as You have loved us.

How does your relationship reflect two becoming one?

EXPRESSION OF LOVE

"Out of the abundance of the heart
the mouth speaks."
MATTHEW 12:34 NKJV

Communication exposes what is going on inside your heart.
If your heart, your internal reality, is governed by fear, then
you are going to telegraph that through your body language,
facial expressions, words, and tone. Conversely, if your heart is
governed by faith, hope, and love, you will release this reality
through what you say and how you say it.

You cannot hide what is going on in your heart for very long.
It will be evident in the way you speak to each other or act
toward one another. When you choose to love from the deepest
place in your heart, that is what you will communicate to your
spouse.

*God, You have such incredible love and mercy for us. Help us to
be forgiving and kind to each other. We want to communicate
love at every turn, and that means it needs to be in our hearts.
You are the author of love—the very definition of it. As we spend
time with You, may our love for each other increase.*

*When you communicate with each other,
what are your hearts expressing?*

PRETENDING

Let us then approach God's throne of grace with confidence,
so that we may receive mercy and find grace to help us
in our time of need.

HEBREWS 4:16 NIV

If your heart is governed by fear, then much of what you
communicate is designed to hide what is really going on inside.
You hold back, pretend something doesn't hurt, or act happy
when your heart is breaking in an attempt to avoid the pain
that being real can inflict.

You or your spouse may never have been taught how to
interpret and translate the language of your thoughts,
emotions, and desires into words, let alone communicate them
to each other. As a result, your internal realities have never
been validated. Because this creates shame and fear, you hide
behind an acceptable social mask. This is of no benefit to your
connection. You must both learn how to let each other in to see
what is going on in your hearts.

*God, help us to be real with how we are feeling. We don't want to
pretend we are ok and happy when we aren't. Give us the tools
we need to communicate openly and honestly with ourselves
and with each other.*

How can you be real with each other?

THE GREAT HIJACKER

"I am the way, and the truth, and the life;
no one comes to the Father except through Me."
JOHN 14:6 NASB

Fear of truth is the great hijacker of communication. When you don't have either the courage or the ability to face the truth of what you feel, think, and need, you end up communicating confusing and inaccurate information—sometimes even downright falsehoods.

If you never really learn to value and understand what's going on inside of you, how can you value and understand what is going on with your spouse? If you don't know yourself, you can't get to know your spouse—someone with a completely different experience and perspective than you—and value the truth of who they are.

Jesus, You are the way, the truth, and the life. Thank You for providing a way to the Father. Give us the courage we need to face the truth of what we feel, think, and need, so we can value ourselves and each other rightly.

Are you allowing the fear of truth to hijack your communication?

VALUED AND UNDERSTOOD

Above all, guard the affections of your heart,
for they affect all that you are.
Pay attention to the welfare of your innermost being,
for from there flows the wellspring of life.

PROVERBS 4:23 TPT

Only those who value and understand themselves can value
and understand others. Only those who can communicate
honestly with themselves can communicate honestly with
others. These are both the traits of a powerful person.

Unless you become a powerful person who values what is
going on in your heart, your experience with communication
is guaranteed to be an endless sequence of misunderstandings
and being misunderstood.

*God, You love us so perfectly and completely. Thank You for
understanding our humanity and our internal struggles. Show
us how to communicate honestly with ourselves and others so
we can avoid misunderstanding whenever possible.*

What is the welfare of your innermost being?

FEAR STYLES

You desire truth in the innermost being,
And in secret You will make wisdom known to me.

PSALM 51:6 NASB

Powerless people communicate out of the fear of truth,
and they primarily do it in one of three styles: passive
communication, aggressive communication, or passive-
aggressive communication. Each of these styles traces back
to false core beliefs about the value of what is inside. Worse,
these styles cultivate fear and destroy connection because they
provide a way for people not to tell the truth.

If you or your spouse tend to communicate in one of these
styles, you might want to consider how much you truly value
yourself. As you choose to communicate the truth, you will
become more powerful and your communication with your
spouse will improve dramatically.

*God, You want us to be truthful at our core. We don't want to
fall into the trap of communicating out of fear. Give us wisdom
to speak honestly what is on our hearts and minds.*

How do you typically communicate?

PASSIVE COMMUNICATION

*The king is pleased with words from righteous lips;
he loves those who speak honestly.*

PROVERBS 16:13 NLT

Passive communicators attempt to convince the world that everyone else is more important than they are. Their core belief is, "Others matter, but I don't." When faced with a joint decision in a relationship, the passive person insists that the other person's thoughts, feelings, and needs matter more. If they believe they are being disrespected, they will simply try to absorb it and move on.

If you or your spouse is a passive communicator, you may find yourself saying things like, "Oh, whatever you want. No, that's okay. It didn't hurt. I'm fine. I know you were just upset. I don't need to talk about this anymore. I'm good." You need to learn how to value yourself and speak truthfully about what is going on in your heart. Honest communication will bring closer connection.

Creator God, You have made us equals. You value us as Your treasured possession. Help us to each see ourselves as being important in this relationship. We matter to each other, and we matter to You.

Do you believe that you are valuable?

LIVING A LIE

> "Whoever desires to love life
> and see good days,
> let him keep his tongue from evil
> and his lips from speaking deceit."
>
> 1 PETER 3:10 ESV

Sometimes passive people justify devaluing themselves by painting themselves as long-suffering, patient servants who keep the peace and don't ever make problems. They may even think it's right to have no needs or requirements, but they are living a lie.

Are you afraid of what your spouse will do if they find out you have needs? Maybe you think you will be punished for telling the truth, or you think you might be misinterpreted as being selfish. Somehow, you believe it is noble to hide yourself from the relationship. You have to understand that this only feeds your anxiety. To work toward the goal of closeness and connection, you have to allow your spouse to know the truth inside you, so they can deal with the real you and not just a façade.

God, it is hard to open up and share the truth. Help us to see that we are not being noble by hiding our true feelings. We want true peace, and that means sharing honestly with each other as we work toward connectedness.

Do you think silence is always noble?

THE PASSIVE APPROACH

See to it that no one falls short of the grace of God and that no bitter root grows up to cause trouble and defile many.

HEBREWS 12:15 NIV

The passive approach is impossible to maintain in the long term because it is a lie. The bitterness that grows by absorbing other people's selfishness will ultimately make you more miserable than afraid. This may lead to you taking drastic measures that, at first, cause you to feel like your needs are finally being met.

The problem here is that when you allow bitterness to creep into your relationship, you don't see things rightly. Devaluing your own needs can make you just as selfish as the person you are bitter toward. It is more likely you were acting out of self-protection than a desire to benefit others.

Father, forgive us for where we have been selfish. We want to be full of grace toward each other, so You are gracious toward us. Help us to get rid of any bitterness that hinders our connection.

Are you carrying any bitterness toward each other?

A T-REX

Do not think of yourself more highly than you ought, but rather think of yourself with sober judgment, in accordance with the faith God has distributed to each of you.

ROMANS 12:3 NIV

An aggressive communicator is like a T-Rex. Their core belief is that they matter and no one else does. Aggressive communicators know how to get what they want. They are large and in charge because they are the biggest, loudest, scariest person in the room. When a passive communicator and an aggressive communicator are in a relationship together, they both agree that the T-Rex is the only one who matters.

If you and your spouse have this communication dynamic, your anxiety will be through the roof. The unequal value and power balance entirely eliminates intimacy. You will only be in a relationship of survival. Both of these communication methods are motivated by fear and selfishness, and both come from a position of being powerless.

God, You are higher than the highest heavens, and we are mere humans. Help us to have a right perspective of ourselves and others. We want to show equality and give others a chance to communicate honestly with us.

Do you communicate like a T-Rex?

BUT NOT REALLY

Do not lie to one another,
since you stripped off the old self with its evil practices.
COLOSSIANS 3:9 NASB

The passive-aggressive communication style is the most
sophisticated, and therefore the most devious of the fear-
based communication styles. This kind of communicator
believes others matter… but not really. They manipulate and
control through active deceit and subtle-but-deadly forms of
punishment. They are famous for sarcastic innuendos, veiled
threats, manipulative use of Scriptures, judgments that come in
the form of counsel, and withholding love.

If one of you tends to communicate in a passive-aggressive
manner, what you say to someone's face will be very different
than what you are feeling. It's important that you see this form
of communication for what it really is. The health of your
relationship depends on you both being able to communicate
what you are actually thinking and feeling.

*Jesus, help us to be truthful communicators with others and
especially with each other. We don't want to fall into passive-
aggressive behavior that is two-faced and deceitful. Forgive
us for where we have been manipulative and show us how
to change.*

Can you communicate honestly with each other?

MIXED MESSAGES

We are careful to be honorable before the Lord,
but we also want everyone else to see that we are honorable.

2 CORINTHIANS 8:21 NLT

Because passive-aggressive communicators maintain a
veneer of civility, it is often hard for people on the outside to
understand why someone has such a difficult time being in
relationship with them. Someone who is trying to gain counsel
about dealing with a passive-aggressive person looks crazy
because they are the only ones who perceive the hostility and
manipulation.

If you engage in passive-aggressive behavior, you may appear
to be happy and carefree to everyone except your partner.
Don't be someone who behind closed doors becomes critical,
accusatory, silent, or sends mixed messages. These behaviors
are not the kind that build intimacy in your marriage.

*God, we need Your help to be honorable before each other as
much as we are around others. Show us where we are being
passive-aggressive in our behavior and lead us in truth.*

Are you sending mixed messages to each other?

CHOCOLATE DRAGONS

People will be lovers of self, lovers of money, proud, arrogant, abusive, disobedient to their parents, ungrateful, unholy, heartless, unappeasable, slanderous, without self-control, brutal, not loving good, treacherous, reckless, swollen with conceit, lovers of pleasure rather than lovers of God, having the appearance of godliness, but denying its power. Avoid such people.

2 TIMOTHY 3:2-5 ESV

Passive-aggressive communicators could be described as chocolate-covered dragons. On the outside they appear charming and romantic, they flatter incessantly, and they seem too good to be true. It's not until you get into deeper relationships that you learn they are chocolate-covered dragons. Once the nice façade is gone, they become vicious manipulators who discount others' thoughts and feelings. They are often jealous of anything that doesn't revolve around them.

If you see these tendencies in yourself, take a moment to truthfully assess what is going on. You need to take control of yourself and choose to turn your love on. Begin sharing the truth of how you feel and listen to what your spouse needs from you.

Father, we want to change the atmosphere in our home by becoming powerful and being real with ourselves and each other. Help us avoid becoming chocolate-covered dragons.

How are you sharing truth in your home?

ASSERTIVE COMMUNICATION

Your words are so powerful
that they will kill or give life,
and the talkative person will reap the consequences.
PROVERBS 18:21 TPT

What communication style grows out of being powerful and loving the truth? Assertive communication. The core belief of assertive communicators is that both partners in a relationship matter. They refuse to have relationships or conversations where both people do not have a high, equal value. They are not afraid to show the other person what is happening inside them.

When you value what is in you, you take the time and effort to understand your needs, and to find words that express them clearly and honestly. This process enhances your ability to value and understand what your spouse communicates about their heart as well. When you communicate assertively, it shows a core value of honor and mutual respect.

Jesus, thank You for communicating Your love to us in so many ways. Help us to value ourselves in a way that gives us the ability to value each other. We want to form a habit of open communication and honesty with each other.

Do you share what is happening in your hearts with each other?

INSTEAD

Get rid of all bitterness, rage, anger, harsh words, and slander, as well as all types of evil behavior. Instead, be kind to each other, tenderhearted, forgiving one another, just as God through Christ has forgiven you.

EPHESIANS 4:31-32 NLT

When you are an assertive communicator, you are not afraid of being powerful or letting other people be powerful within your relationship or conversation. You refuse to give in to the temptation to turn into a fear-based communicator, and you confront other people if you see them slipping into those roles.

When you encourage powerful behavior and honest communication with your spouse, you are showing movement toward them and a desire for greater connection.

God, give us the strength to confront issues as they arise, and to communicate in a way that shows Your love and grace. Help us to exhibit powerful behavior and honest communication in our relationship.

How can you be an assertive communicator today?

A Good Response

Make every effort to live in peace with everyone and to be
holy; without holiness no one will see the Lord.

HEBREWS 12:14 NIV

As an assertive communicator, you would respond to a passive
person with, "What are you going to do about that?" To an
aggressive person, you would refuse to talk until there was
a show of respect. And to a passive-aggressive individual,
you would say, "We can talk later when you choose to be
responsible and tell me what is really going on."

In other words, you set consistent boundaries around a
conversation so that it stays respectful, and you require both
participants to equally participate in pursuing the goal of the
conversation. When you create this kind of environment in
your home, your communication will be both peaceful and
effective.

*God, living in peace with everyone is quite a task! Thank You
for Your mercy and forgiveness when we fail so miserably. Show
us what it means to be holy in the way we communicate with
others.*

How are you living in peace with everyone?

PRIORITY OF AGREEMENT

Haughtiness goes before destruction;
humility precedes honor.
PROVERBS 18:12 NLT

Talking is not communicating unless it has a goal or purpose. Most often in communication, the goal is agreement. But if the goal is agreement, what happens when you disagree? One person must persuade the other to agree with them. Unfortunately, persuasion has a way of slipping into pressure, manipulation, and control. Having a priority of agreement demands that there really can't be two different people in the conversation—there can only be one.

The longer one person refuses to respond to the other's efforts to convince them to agree, the more anxiety grows in the conversation. Before long, the battle lines are drawn, and you are allowing your need to be right to overtake the need to protect the connection. The conversation becomes a fight over which person has the right perception, the right answer, or the right decision.

God, help us to communicate well. We don't want to manipulate each other into agreement at the expense of our closeness. Let us respond to each other in love and submit our opinions with humility and grace.

What is your typical priority or goal in your communication?

RELATIONSHIP KILLER

A fool takes no pleasure in understanding,
but only in expressing his opinion.
PROVERBS 18:2 ESV

If you aren't careful, it will be only a matter of time before one of you introduces some kind of relationship killer to the conversation. A relationship killer is a message that invalidates or disqualifies someone's thoughts, feelings, or needs in some way. It often happens when someone talks about their feelings, and the other person responds with dismissal, disbelief, or invalidation: "Well, that's not logical." "Feelings aren't reality." "That doesn't even make sense."

Although unintended, the message you communicate to your spouse when you dismiss their feelings is that you are valuable, and they are not. It's as if you are saying that only your perspective is logical, significant, and right. When either of you start devaluing the other's thoughts, feelings, or needs in some way, you attack your connection like a pack of wolves.

God, help us to speak kindly to each other and to listen well. We want to encourage and build each other up instead of tearing down. Show us when we need to change our responses, keeping our love on and pursuing connection.

How do you respond to each other when feelings are shared?

To Understand

Make your ear attentive to wisdom;
Incline your heart to understanding.
PROVERBS 2:2 NASB

If connection is your priority, then your goal of communication cannot be agreement because then one of you has to disappear when there is disagreement. As you know, people do not always agree! If you want to keep two powerful people involved and connected in a conversation, the first goal in the conversation must be to understand.

When your goal is to understand, you say, "I want to understand your unique perspective and experience. I want to understand the truth of what is happening inside you. And I want you to understand the same things about me." If you understand each other's hearts, you can move toward each other in ways that build your connection. You can respond to each other's thoughts, respect feelings, and help meet needs.

Father, You understand each of us better than we understand ourselves or each other. Thank You for Your compassion and grace that You show when we talk with You. Help us to move toward a goal of understanding each other when we communicate. We want to listen like You do.

How good are you at trying to understand where your spouse is coming from?

Radically Different

The one who has knowledge uses words with restraint,
and whoever has understanding is even-tempered.

PROVERBS 17:27 NIV

When you are both powerful, and you decide that your goal
in communicating is to understand each other, you will find
yourselves more involved and connected than you perhaps
thought possible.

The results of your conversations are going to be radically
different than when you were seeking agreement alone.
Pursuing the goal of understanding will help you progress
through increasingly deeper levels of honesty in order to build
true intimacy and trust in a relationship.

*God, we want greater understanding—of You and of each other.
Teach us how to listen with the intention of hearing not only the
words but also the heart. Help us to establish greater trust and
intimacy with each other as we share openly and honestly.*

*What can you do to pursue a goal of understanding
in your communication with each other?*

FACTS AND CLICHÉS

Though good advice lies deep within the heart,
a person with understanding will draw it out.
PROVERBS 20:5 NLT

When you started getting to know each other, your conversations probably centered on the world around you. You would have exchanged facts and clichés like, "How are you?" "Fine, and you?" "Nice day today." "Yes, it's beautiful outside." "Eighty degrees, I hear." You get the point. These conversations require a minimal level of connection or vulnerability; you could probably have them with a stranger. Sadly, there are many people who stick with facts and clichés because it's comfortable and safe.

You or your spouse may have been hurt in a past relationship when trying to graduate to that next level of intimacy in communication. You might have had long, disrespectful, relationship-killer conversations and decided it was safer to retreat to communication that required no vulnerability or risk. You will need to figure out together how to pursue a goal of connection instead of distance in your communication.

God, show us where we need to change how we communicate. Let us begin to trust, so we share more deeply than just passing along information.

Have you graduated from the fact and clichés stage of communication in your relationship?

HEART COMMUNICATION

Discretion will watch over you,
Understanding will guard you,
To rescue you from the way of evil.
<small>PROVERBS 2:11-12 NASB</small>

The only way you can build a heart-to-heart connection together is to communicate on a heart level about your feelings and needs. This is the level where you express vulnerability and build trust, where you get in touch with the truth about who you are and how you affect people around you.

It is possible that you experience a disconnect every day when you try to communicate. Sometimes there is a lot going on around you that you don't always pick up. You may be completely unaware of how other people experience you. The person who knows and understands you best can likely enlighten you about how you come across if you are both willing to be honest with each other.

God, You communicate Your heart to us so well, and You see what is going on in each of us. Help us to be aware of how we affect those around us. We want to build a heart-to-heart connection.

How can you communicate on a heart level with each other?

Auto Response

Let the wise listen and add to their learning,
and let the discerning get guidance.

PROVERBS 1:5 NIV

There is probably a recurring argument that crops up in your relationship. When that reaction is triggered, you may wonder why your spouse doesn't just calm down and be more like you. How they respond may seem completely illogical, but you cannot force them to feel what you feel or know what you know. When they respond a certain way, try to assess it at a feeling level.

If you argue with feelings, you devalue each other. You are essentially telling your spouse that there is no good reason for them to feel the way they do. Operating this way in your relationship is as ridiculous as responding to someone's statement of being hungry with, "No, you're not. I'm not hungry, so how could you be?" You have to learn how to respond to others by taking the time to understand, appreciate, and validate their feelings.

God, give us the grace to listen patiently to each other when we share our feelings. We want to understand one another on a deeper level that communicates our love and care.

How can you respond better to your spouse's feelings?

WHAT YOU NEED

"Your Father already knows what you need
before you ask him."
MATTHEW 6:8 TPT

When you learn how to value each other's feelings, you will
not only make it safe to communicate those feelings with each
other, but you will also listen and respond. You will be inviting
your spouse to go deeper, showing what it is that they need,
so you can move from understanding to decision-making and
action.

Understanding one another's needs is the Holy Grail of
communication. If you can find out what your spouse needs in
a conversation, and figure out how to satisfy that need, it will
change everything!

*Father, You know everything we need before we even ask.
We aren't there yet! Please help us to listen with a desire to
understand and fulfill each other's needs.*

*How difficult is it to understand what your spouse truly needs?
How can you help each other move to understanding more quickly?*

SIMPLY ASK

O Lord, all my longing is before you;
my sighing is not hidden from you.
PSALM 38:9 ESV

The faster you can get to the question of what your spouse
needs, the faster you can start doing something about it. If you
or your spouse are not used to being listened to, you might not
know what you need, or how to communicate it. You could
think you have to present a solid case in order for your spouse
to help, agree with, or change for you.

Your spouse may be thrown off guard when you simply show
up with the question, "What do you need? Tell me so I can help
you with that." It might never have crossed their mind that
you would help simply because they need something. Once
they experience this level of understanding, they immediately
recognize it as a practice of intimacy. They feel cared for and
loved, which casts out anxiety and helps the search for the
truth of what their heart really needs.

*God, thank You for patience: a gift of Your Holy Spirit that
we can ask for often. Help us to communicate our care and
willingness to help each other in discovering what we need.*

How difficult is it for each of you to communicate what you need?

BE REAL

The heart of the righteous ponders how to answer,
But the mouth of the wicked pours out evil things.
PROVERBS 15:28 NASB

You can start practicing the skills of assertive communication
by paying attention to your thoughts, feelings, and needs
and respecting the value of those. Then start doing the same
for your spouse. Check yourself when you are tempted to
invalidate their experience or heart. Listen with the purpose of
understanding—especially understanding what they are feeling
and what they need.

Seek healing from past experiences that have led you to fear
the truth of your heart and made you a passive, aggressive, or
passive-aggressive communicator. Be real with yourself. If you
start slipping into your old styles of communication, then do
what needs to be done to make things right.

*Jesus, You knew just what to say in every situation. You
understood the heart of every person You engaged with. Show
us how to stop and ponder before answering—even before
answering ourselves. Let us be real about what our hearts need.*

How can you pay better attention
to your thoughts, feelings, and needs?

IMPART UNDERSTANDING

The unfolding of your words gives light;
it imparts understanding to the simple.
PSALM 119:130 ESV

When you commit to becoming the best communicator you can possibly be, you commit to connection and to being a truly powerful person. Not only will your relationship with your heart change for the better, but your relationships with others will be transformed as well.

With both of you working toward the goal of communicating with the intention of truly understanding each other, you will find a deeper level of connection and closeness. You will begin to trust each other with your hearts and be honest about your needs.

Father, thank You for Your wisdom and guidance in our marriage. Help us to turn to Your Word for the understanding we need. Give us strength to trust each other and love well.

How can you increase your level of trust?

SEASONED WITH SALT

Let your conversation be always full of grace, seasoned with salt, so that you may know how to answer everyone.

COLOSSIANS 4:6 NIV

Although it should be pretty simple, communication seems to break down far too easily. It is a fragile process to be sure, but it has been made more complex than it needs to be. In its most basic definition, communication is the effective transfer of information from one person to another.

When you communicate with each other, you need to seek understanding. That should be the goal. Forget trying to be in agreement; that won't happen all the time and it only leads to one person not feeling properly valued. When you try to understand each other, you are moving closer together instead of further away.

Jesus, You understand every person and You communicate with such grace and mercy when we are honest about our hearts. Help us to follow Your example of love.

How can you season your conversations with salt?

HE HEARS

The righteous cry out, and the LORD hears,
And delivers them out of all their troubles.
PSALM 34:17 NKJV

Most people experience the feeling of not being heard or understood at least once in their lives. For some, it happens so frequently they begin to shut down. Why share feelings or intimacy with someone if it only leads to heartache? It is painful when you feel like you aren't being listened to or heard, especially when you are trying hard to communicate.

If your spouse doesn't appear to hear a word you say, you may feel like giving up on saying anything at all. More angst is created when the only words heard are those that are being used against you to support their argument. Remember, your point in communication should be to understand, not to agree.

God, thank You for always hearing us. Help us to listen to each other and encourage healthy communication that shows honor and love.

How can you help make your spouse feel heard?

UNSEARCHABLE

Do you not know? Have you not heard?
The Everlasting God, the LORD,
the Creator of the ends of the earth
Does not become weary or tired.
His understanding is unsearchable.

ISAIAH 40:28 NASB

The goal of understanding is practiced by listening. You may think communication is about speaking, but the greatest skill you could ever cultivate in your relationship is to listen well. It is especially important to listen in the middle of a disagreement.

As a listener, you need to be calm, caring, and honest, and sometimes this means hearing things about yourself that aren't pleasant. The judgments may not even be right. But if you seek to understand each other through the disagreement, you allow an opportunity for each person to feel heard, known, and valued.

God, Your understanding of each of us is unsearchable. You know what is going on in our hearts even when our mouths are saying something different. Help us to be good listeners.

What could you do to be a better listener?

RIGHT JUDGMENT

"I can do nothing on my own. As I hear, I judge,
and my judgment is just, because I seek not my own will
but the will of him who sent me."

JOHN 5:30 ESV

You can think about being an effective communicator as if you have to explain what color you are on the inside. Others can't see what it's like in your mind, so you have to tell them. They may have never guessed you were orange or blue; it's your job to tell them.

If your spouse doesn't know who you really are, it will be very difficult for them to make good decisions regarding you. The same is true the other way. If you don't know your spouse, you won't make good judgments about them either. Even if you think you are an excellent judge, you cannot be accurate if you don't have the right information. You understand each other by telling one another about yourselves. In your most intimate relationship, you must trust each other enough to share the sensitive, vulnerable information about who you are.

God, You are the perfect judge. We cannot even begin to know all that is going on inside of every person we meet. But You do. Help us to seek Your heart for each other so we can see rightly.

How can you build your trust with each other?

NO GUESSING

Never let loyalty and kindness leave you!
Tie them around your neck as a reminder.
Write them deep within your heart.
Then you will find favor with both God and people,
and you will earn a good reputation.

PROVERBS 3:3-4 NLT

On the pillar of trust, the exchange of truth is how you are going to get each other the best possible information to make the best possible decisions for your relationship. It's important that you send the right message, which should be a constant message that you care about your spouse and about your marriage.

When you are disconnected, don't start to think it's okay to make each other guess whether or not that's true. Good communication that shows how much you both care about each other keeps anxiety low and your time together pleasurable.

God, You don't make us guess whether You love us. You show us in so many ways every day. Teach us how to be more like You in our relationship with each other.

How can you show your spouse you care?

BOTH MATTER

"These things dominate the thoughts of unbelievers all over the world, but your Father already knows our needs."

LUKE 12:30 NLT

You both have needs. It's important that each of you recognize and embrace this truth. Don't try to convince yourself that everyone else has needs and you don't. That creates a passive communicator. Both parties in this marriage matter, and both need to trust each other enough to be vulnerable about their needs.

The only thing you will accomplish by continuing with the façade of not having needs is to let a root of bitterness grow between you. Don't be afraid of putting demands on your relationship. That makes it healthy. Say what you need and listen to what your spouse needs too.

Father, we matter to You. You have made that clear in Your Word. Thank You for Your care for us in all areas of our lives. Help us to share what we need with each other in a gentle way and teach us how to respond in love.

What do you need from each other today?

GREATER CONCERN

Abandon every display of selfishness. Possess a greater concern
for what matters to others instead of your own interests.
PHILIPPIANS 2:4 TPT

Are you okay with your spouse having needs? Do you feel you
are equally important? You may not even realize that your
inability to see your spouse's needs communicates that you
don't care. It makes you seem selfish and mean. But it could be
that you are afraid. You don't want to be vulnerable because if
your needs aren't met, you will be disappointed and hurt.

Don't be an aggressive communicator. Listen to your own
needs and listen to the needs of your spouse. Communicate
honestly with love and patience. Show your spouse that you
care about their needs. Move toward each other and keep your
love on.

*God, forgive us for where we have been self-centered and focused
only on our own needs. We want to serve each other in love and
create a safe place to share our needs with each other.*

How can you turn your focus to your spouse?

IN THE MOMENT

The LORD detests lying lips,
but he delights in people who are trustworthy.
PROVERBS 12:22 NIV

If sarcasm marks a high percentage of your dialogue, you may be a passive-aggressive communicator. What you convey to others can be very confusing. They think they matter, but suddenly they don't. You can carry out a conversation that seems successful, but you leave filled with anger or bitterness. You don't communicate honesty in the moment; you do that behind the scenes.

Communicating this way with your spouse builds the relationship on fear. You won't allow them to see inside of you, so they don't know who you truly are. It is important for your connection that you figure out how to speak honestly, boldly, and kindly with each other. This will help reduce anxiety in your relationship.

God, help us both to be real with our feelings and our words. We want to speak to each other honestly in the moment and not operate in a passive-aggressive manner. Guide us in Your truth and kindness.

How much sarcasm is in your dialogue with others?

CULTIVATE HONOR

The reward of humility and the fear of the LORD
Are riches, honor, and life.

PROVERBS 22:4 NASB

The best way for you to communicate in your marriage is
to be assertive. This requires both partners to be powerful.
Both of you will allow and require the other to be powerful.
Relationships work better when aggressive communicators are
limited, passive communicators are forced to talk, and passive-
aggressive communicators are called out.

You can both begin to send messages that what each of you
think, say, need, and feel matter. As two powerful people, you
have an opportunity to cultivate honor together: working
through relational conflict and disagreement, exchanging the
truth, and taking responsibility for yourselves.

*Jesus, You humbled Yourself in the biggest way possible. We
want to be assertive with each other but also speak in a way that
is honoring. Help us to get rid of old habits of communication
that are damaging.*

What message are you currently communicating with your spouse?

A DEEPER LEVEL

Out of your reverence for Christ
be supportive of each other in love.
EPHESIANS 5:21 TPT

You can have cliché and fact conversations with complete
strangers. "I slept well." "God is good." "It's raining." They require
zero vulnerability in the exchange. This level of communication
is the least intimate and demands very little skill.

The next level is different. You and your spouse have different
opinions, perspectives, ideas, or information. Now your
communication skills are going to be tested. When your spouse
says something and you think, *I disagree. I don't think that
way,* what do you do? These thoughts can chase you into an
argument. But if you can have a respectful conversation about
an issue, you will break through the superficial level and begin
communicating on deeper levels.

*God, we understand that we aren't going to agree on everything
in life. Help us to be able to disagree well, and to make each
other feel heard and loved in spite of our differences of opinion.*

What typically happens when you disagree with each other?

A DIFFERENT EXPERIENCE

Clothe yourselves with humility toward one another.
1 PETER 5:5 NIV

Do you find yourselves settling for superficial levels rather than growing in your communication skills? Once you're willing to allow each other to be yourselves in your relationship, you begin to view your differences in a new way. You see your spouse's life experience as being different than yours and that may be a strange feeling for you.

Some people say that feelings don't matter, or the only thing that matters is what the Bible says. But how does that work? When your spouse says they are cold, do you say, "No, you're not. The Bible doesn't say you are cold"? You can't tell your partner how to feel, and when you try to answer their heart with your head, it hurts. They didn't tell you how they were feeling so you could correct it; they told you so you would know who they are in this moment.

Father, help us not to be dismissive of each other when our experiences are different. We don't want to start telling each other how to feel; we want to learn more about one another, so our connection deepens.

How can you grow in your communication skills?

NOT THE SAME

I will praise You, for I am fearfully and wonderfully made;
Marvelous are Your works,
And that my soul knows very well.

PSALM 139:14 NKJV

A lot of the time you and your spouse don't need the same thing. When you get down to the deepest level of communication, you can realize that without it being a threat. It's the challenge of effective communication.

Your spouse may not realize how desperately you need someone just to listen to you. You might not know what is going on inside of you, but if someone asks what you need, it can change the course of the whole conversation. This type of communication sends a message that says, "I care about what you need."

God, You always care about what we need. You know even better than we do, and You understand with knowledge that far surpasses the greatest wisdom we possess. Thank You for Your patience and care.

How quickly can you get to a "what do you need" question in your conversations?

IT IS GOOD

He who finds a wife finds what is good
and receives favor from the LORD.

PROVERBS 18:22 NIV

Getting married means two people coming together from
different families, friend groups, and experiences in life. You
and your spouse should step back and look at your relationship
with all these different people coming together so you can have
healthy expectations.

You are both from different situations. When you merge, there
is naturally going to be some anxiety and issues will come up
probably sooner rather than later. Knowing this ahead of time
and having the tools to be able to communicate in order to stay
connected through the anxiety or challenges, could make all
the difference.

*God, thank You for our marriage. Thank You for giving us this
relationship to bless us, and not to be a source of anxiety or
stress in our lives. We trust You for the best. We want to learn
how to keep our love on and move toward each other, instead
of away, when differences arise.*

How different are your backgrounds?

ABILITY TO TRUST

"If you cause one of these little ones who trusts in me to fall
into sin, it would be better for you to have a large millstone tied
around your neck and be drowned in the depths of the sea."

MATTHEW 18:6 NLT

You were designed to live out of trust. Psychologists argue that
trust is the first developmental task every person must achieve
in infancy in order to develop a healthy sense of personhood
and to make and maintain healthy relationships.

Jesus said it is better for someone to tie an enormous rock
around your neck, kick you into the deepest part of the ocean,
and let you sink, rather than allow you to cause a child to
stumble. Apparently, protecting the trust of the vulnerable is
a big deal to Him—and for good reason. When people mess
with your trust at an early age, you are likely to struggle in life.
Most gang members, high school dropouts, and addicts had
bad childhoods. Most abusers were abused. Most divorcées
had divorced parents. Affairs, selfishness, self-inflicted pain,
and walls of protection all stem from broken trust during
childhood.

*God, You keep Your word. You never break Your promises; You
always do what You say You will do. Help us to be more like
You in this.*

How has your childhood affected your ability to trust?

A TRUST CYCLE

In my desperation I prayed, and the LORD listened;
he saved me from all my troubles.
PSALM 34:6 NLT

The minute you were born, you came out of the womb asking
if you could trust the world. Your little heart and mind needed
to know. The answer to this question came as your primary
caregiver met—or failed to meet—your physical and emotional
needs.

Babies, like anyone else, have needs. In fact, needs are about all a
baby has. And the only thing babies can do to let the world know
what they need is to cry. They cry when they are hungry or tired,
when they need a diaper changed, when they need to burp, and
when they need to be held. When they cry and a need is met, a
trust cycle is completed. They learn they can trust themselves,
because the signals they are sending are being understood, and
they learn to trust the person meeting their needs.

*Father, we trust You with all of our needs. Thank You for paying
such close attention to us. When we cry out to You, You hear us,
and You interpret our needs perfectly.*

*Were your primary needs met as an infant? Who was the most
consistent in completing trust cycles with you as a child?*

THE FULL RANGE

The LORD redeems the life of his servants;
none of those who take refuge in him will be condemned.

PSALM 34:22 ESV

A trust cycle can only be completed through a relational connection because only a relationship can meet the full range of your needs. The same is true for babies. If they are fed, clothed, and washed, but never experience prolonged human touch, cuddling, and face-to-face contact with their primary caregiver, their brains, personalities, and capacity for bonding will remain underdeveloped, and in some cases permanently stunted.

Whether you want to admit it or not, both you and your spouse are looking for love. You want to engage in mutual connection and experience your need for love being met. As you and your spouse complete more and more trust cycles, your bond becomes stronger.

Jesus, You are the most trustworthy person to have ever walked the earth. Help us to trust You more and depend on You to take care of us. Completing trust cycles with You brings spiritual growth and maturity.

How is your capacity for bonding? What can you do to enhance it?

UNBROKEN TRUST

The LORD is near to all who call on Him,
To all who call on Him in truth.
PSALM 145:18 NASB

The deepest human need is to love and be loved and to
engage in lasting relational bonds. The ability to meet this
need develops as trust cycles are consistently achieved in
interactions with others. A trust cycle is completed when you
have a need, express the need, have someone respond to the
need, and satisfy the need.

The trust cycle can break down at any point. Trust is damaged
if you or your spouse fail to identify or express your needs. It
takes a hit if neither of you respond (or respond negatively)
when a need is expressed. If the need is not eventually met,
trust is also broken.

*Father, You care for us perfectly. Whenever we come to You,
You listen and act. Your cycle of trust is never broken. Help us
to share what we need and help us to listen to each other's needs.*

What is your need right now?

SHINE THE LIGHT

The light shines in the darkness,
and the darkness has not overcome it.
JOHN 1:5 ESV

You will experience broken trust in life. Both you and your
spouse probably faced it in childhood simply because all
parents, even the best of them, are human beings who make
mistakes and bring their own areas of brokenness into
parenting. If these wounds are not healed and truth and trust
restored, they will fester, damaging your ability to create
intimacy in your relationships.

Painful experiences give way to wounds that fester when you
agree with lies that say God doesn't love you, no one loves you,
there's something wrong with you, you are unworthy of love,
you don't deserve to have your needs met, etc. These lies create
an expectation for unmet needs, which leads to more painful,
disappointing experiences, and prevents the wounds from
healing.

*God, destroy the lies in our hearts and minds with Your truth.
You love us deeply. You care for us with the greatest affection
imaginable. Meet us with Your healing power, so we can begin
to trust again.*

Where do you need healing from broken trust?

HEALING CYCLES

The LORD is trustworthy in all he promises
and faithful in all he does.
PSALM 145:13 NIV

If you have gone through counseling or inner healing, you
know how one bad experience or one empowered lie can
bring significant pain and relational handicaps into your life. If
either of you grew up in environments where you consistently
experienced neglect or punishment in response to your needs,
the damage is significant.

The cycle of mistrust creates an alienating, painful reality
where you may feel hopeless about ever having your needs
met because you are unable to trust others or form strong
relational connections. You and your spouse can work together
to complete trust cycles consistently. This will help the process
of healing and bring closer connection.

*Father, Your faithfulness is unmatched. What You promise, You
fulfill. You promise to always be with us. We need You to help us
build trust together. Give us the grace to move toward each other
even in our own pain. You will heal and restore us.*

*How can you begin completing cycles of trust
in your relationship?*

WORTHY OF LOVE

Lord, your endless love stretches
from one eternity to the other,
unbroken and unrelenting toward those who fear you.
PSALM 103:17 TPT

When you are cut off from love, you become a survivor, and that has its own set of problems. If you or your spouse are a survivor, you have probably learned to manipulate your environment and other people to get some of your needs met. After years of abandonment, neglect, and abuse, you believe you are unworthy of love. You don't expect relationships to last—why should you? It's never been safe for you to trust or be vulnerable, and you don't have the emotional resources to meet anyone else's needs. So, you take what you can get.

When you create this kind of reality, where you are unloved, unable to be in relationships, and have unmet needs that cause you pain, you are destroying your opportunity for a satisfying life. God sent His Son to deliver you from being an orphan. Don't walk this life alone. Let your spouse love you. Let them in. Share vulnerably with them and begin to trust.

God, help us not to agree with the orphan spirit in our lives and relationships. We want to love and be loved. We believe You for greater intimacy and trust.

How can you fight against the orphan spirit in your relationship?

START OVER

"If anyone causes one of these little ones—those who believe in me—to stumble, it would be better for them if a large millstone were hung around their neck and they were thrown into the sea."

MARK 9:42 NIV

Jesus' comment about how serious it is to cause a child to stumble reveals the jealous, protective love of the Father for His lost, orphaned children, which includes everyone. Jesus went to the cross to avenge the stolen innocence and broken trust you inherited after the Fall. When He declared that we all had to be born again, He was intending to start the trust cycles over again.

He placed you in the Father's arms, where you will experience unconditional love, acceptance, and care. He will meet your needs when you cry out to Him—especially your need to be loved. You will learn how to trust again, and you will be able to build relationships with Him and with one another. You and your spouse can have a marriage where both hearts will be satisfied. It is possible with God.

Jesus, thank You for Your work on the cross that gave us access to a relationship with the Father. We can experience perfect trust cycles over and over again with You. We look to You today to fill our hearts with the love and acceptance we both need.

What does a trust cycle with God look like to you?

STRONG BOND

I have trusted in your steadfast love;
my heart shall rejoice in your salvation.
PSALM 13:5 ESV

Expressing your needs and building relational connections are
closely intertwined in fact, they are completely dependent on
one another. The level of communication you need to reach to
build a strong relational connection is the level where you and
your spouse express your needs to one another. This is where the
trust cycle begins. You can't build a strong bond of trust without
being able to communicate and meet one another's needs.

If either one of you cannot communicate your needs to the
other clearly, it is going to be very difficult for your spouse
to meet your needs. One of the primary tasks of reaching
maturity is learning how to express your thoughts, feelings,
and needs. You cannot expect your relationship to function
without it.

*God, help us to know ourselves well enough that we can
articulate what it is that we need. Give us the patience we need
to begin to interpret those needs and meet them for each other.*

How well do you each communicate your needs?

NO TELEPATHY

"Your heavenly Father already knows all your needs."
MATTHEW 6:32 NLT

Are either of you guilty of thinking that if your spouse loves you, they should already know what you need? How about expecting each other to notice what bothers you? Where does the desire or expectation that loved ones have a telepathic ability to know our feelings and needs come from? It comes from powerlessness and fear.

Powerless people dream that everything will turn out magically without actually having to communicate. They want to win the lottery, get their dream mate with minimal effort, lose weight without exercise, and have their needs met without ever having to say a word. If you are powerless, you need to hear this: *It doesn't work that way.* You must learn to communicate.

Father, even though You know everything we need before we ask, the same is not true in our earthly relationships. Help us begin to understand the need for good communication in our marriage.

Do you expect your spouse to know what you need without you asking?

A NECESSARY EXPRESSION

> My God will supply all your needs
> according to His riches in glory in Christ Jesus.
>
> PHILIPPIANS 4:19 NASB

The reason you can't get your needs met without expressing them is that you were designed to have your needs met through a relational exchange. God made you that way. This is how He meets your needs.

God, the only one in the universe who knows all things and knows you incomparably better than you know yourself, never says, "Well, obviously I know your needs, so you don't need to tell me about them." Instead, He repeatedly tells you to ask Him for what you need, and gives you some of the most profound, beautiful, and honest language for doing so—like the Lord's Prayer, and most of the Psalms. He won't meet your needs outside of a connection where you have to show up and crack your heart open to Him, because that very connection is what you need to have your needs met in the first place.

Father, thank You that You want to hear from us. You want to know what is on our hearts and minds. You care about our deepest needs, and You can satisfy like none other. Help us to work on our connection with You.

What have you asked God for lately?

No Assumptions

Fools base their thoughts on foolish assumptions,
so their conclusions will be wicked madness.
ECCLESIASTES 10:13 NLT

If God Himself respects your prerogative as an individual to
make your feelings, needs, and desires known to Him in a
relationship, then you may take it that this is how He designed
you to relate with others, including your spouse.

In a respectful relationship, each of you understands you are
responsible to know what is going on inside yourself and to
communicate it to the other person. You don't expect them
to know what is going on, nor will you allow them to assume
they know it. And the opposite is also true: you won't make
assumptions about what is going on in your spouse.

*Father, help us to communicate our needs to each other. Remind
us that it is our responsibility to tell each other what is going on
inside us and help us to care enough to ask what is going on in
one another.*

*How can you stay away from assuming your spouse
knows what is going on inside of you?*

FUZZY LINES

Do not be rash with your mouth,
And let not your heart utter anything hastily before God.
For God is in heaven, and you on earth;
Therefore let your words be few.

ECCLESIASTES 5:2 NKJV

The belief that other people can know you, or that you can know others, without needing to willingly disclose your hearts to one another, is inherently disrespectful and will lead you to act in ways that damage trust.

As long as you believe this, the line of demarcation between your life and your spouse's will remain fuzzy, leading you to avoid taking responsibility for communicating what is going on inside you and to wrongly take responsibility for telling them what is going on inside them. Don't allow this wrong belief to infect your relational communication. Become powerful and take responsibility for yourself only. Communicate what is on your heart and listen as your spouse communicates what is on theirs.

God, give us the strength to take responsibility for our own communication. We need Your help to stay in our zones and reject the belief that we should know each other without disclosing our hearts.

How fuzzy is the line between each of your lives?

DUEL OF JUDGMENTS

A gentle tongue is a tree of life,
but perverseness in it breaks the spirit.
PROVERBS 15:4 ESV

When you and your spouse begin to tell each other what the other is thinking, feeling, or needing, the comments will likely be inherently judgmental, presumptuous, and disrespectful, even if they are offered in a kind tone and with the best of intentions. Unless the person on the receiving end of such comments knows how to set a boundary with disrespect, they will usually go into self-protective mode and either shut down or begin retaliating.

The ensuing duel of judgments is sure to damage your relational connection. If you want to protect your connection and build trust by always communicating respectfully, then your guiding rule must be: "It's my job to tell you about me, and your job to tell me about you."

God, help us to steer clear of making wrong and hurtful judgments about each other. We want to build closeness, not damage our connection. Show us how to be respectful in our communication.

How can you protect your connection and build trust?

THE I MESSAGE

The LORD is with me;
I will not be afraid.
PSALM 118:6 NIV

The best tool for telling your spouse about you is an "I message." The basic structure of the I message is this: "I feel [emotion] when [describe experience] and I need to feel [emotion]." Notice that the I message begins with "I feel," and not "I think." It is designed to let your spouse know what is happening inside you, not for you to let them know what you think about them or what you think they need to do.

As you construct an I message, make sure that you are really expressing a feeling, not an opinion. If you start to say, "I feel *like...*" stop and check yourself. Likely what is going to follow is not a feeling but a judgment. A judgment statement is an expression of mistrust; it says you are too afraid to show your spouse what is really going on inside of you. If this is the case, you are probably looking for your spouse to agree with your assessment of what is wrong with them, and then you'll want them to promise to never be like that again. This will not help your connection.

Father, give us the grace to communicate our feelings without opinions and judgments. Help us to pause and think before we speak.

How well do you communicate I messages?

CONVERSATION HIJACKING

Fools give full vent to their rage,
but the wise bring calm in the end.
PROVERBS 29:11 NIV

Nothing guarantees raising your spouse's defenses or hijacking a conversation more than a judgment statement. In your fear, you convince yourself you can make them change without you needing to be vulnerable, rather than trusting them to change by offering vulnerability.

You may have tried to have a conversation where you asked your spouse if the two of you could share your hearts and speak without defensiveness. You may have even said something about sharing the truth in love. But the minute a judgment statement comes out of one of your mouths, the conversation is over. No one is looking to be told what is wrong with them. The response is never a good one.

Father, it's really difficult to be vulnerable and trust. Help us to give up our need to point out the flaws in each other in an effort to make change happen. Only You can do that kind of work in our lives.

What does it really mean to share the truth in love?

TRUE EMOTIONS

"What comes out of the mouth proceeds from the heart,
and this defiles a person."
MATTHEW 15:18 ESV

In order to be heard, take the approach that says you feel a feeling and it's connected to an event. You tell your spouse when something happened, this is the feeling you had, and you need to feel something different. Maybe you feel hurt when your spouse talks to you a certain way. Or maybe you feel judged by how they frame a question. Or perhaps when they hit the wall when they are angry, it makes you feel afraid. You might feel rejected when they react to your efforts to help.

When you send I messages that are actual feelings connected to events, you let your spouse see your true emotions. Then they can decide how to respond. You become vulnerable and powerful because you protect their choice to move toward you and meet your needs on their own terms.

God, help us to be truly vulnerable with each other. Help us to give words to the feelings we have in our moments of strong emotion. Give us grace to respond well when feelings are shared.

Are you able to connect feelings with events and share them?

HONORING VULNERABILITY

Even a fool, when he keeps silent, is considered wise;
When he closes his lips, he is considered prudent.
PROVERBS 17:28 NASB

If you're on the receiving end of an I message, you have some decisions to make. Will you honor the vulnerability offered, value your spouse's need, and figure out how you can meet it? Are you going to be powerful enough to adjust yourself in order to move toward your partner and protect your connection and trust?

Saying yes to both of these choices often requires at least as much vulnerability as it took for your spouse to show you their need. It is vulnerable (scary and humbling) to allow their needs to influence your heart and your actions. But know this—doing your part to complete the trust cycle is just as important for you as it is for your spouse.

God, we need You to help us keep our hearts tender toward each other. It isn't easy to hear that our actions are causing pain. We want to walk in humility and be willing to change in order to move toward each other.

How well do you complete trust cycles with each other?

NEED FOR NEED

"If you give even a cup of cold water to one of the least of my followers, you will surely be rewarded."
MATTHEW 10:42 NLT

Believe it or not, one of your needs in your relationship with your spouse is to be able to meet their needs. You need them to receive your love. And you need to know that you are a powerful, trustworthy person who can choose to grow, change, and adjust.

It will do wonders for your self-respect when you figure out what you need to do to love people in ways that they can receive it.

Father, You love us so perfectly. You know what we need, and You love to meet our needs when we ask You. Show us how to love each other in the ways we need it the most. Thank You, Jesus, for Your human example of love when You walked this earth. You have given us everything we need to love well.

Do you know how to love each other well?

Paradise

Now we see things imperfectly, like puzzling reflections in a mirror, but then we will see everything with perfect clarity. All that I know now is partial and incomplete, but then I will know everything completely, just as God now knows me completely.

1 Corinthians 13:12 nlt

A safe place for intimacy is created when both of you can express your needs and consistently complete the trust cycle for each other in your relationship. Intimacy—into-me-see—is created between two people who can be themselves together because you can see into each other.

The experience of intimacy—of being completely known and accepted, and completely knowing and accepting in return—is the most satisfying experience you can have in life. Intimacy in a safe place brings euphoria. Remember the Garden of Eden? Paradise was the place where a man and a woman were free to be vulnerable and intimate with one another in every way.

You know us completely, Father. You see into each of us, and You love us regardless of our imperfections and areas of weakness. We want to know and love as You do. Help us to be accepting of each other as we become more intimate.

How good are you at being yourselves with each other?

COVER UP

"I heard you in the garden, and I was afraid
because I was naked; so I hid."

GENESIS 3:10 NIV

Most people are scared to death to be vulnerable in
relationships. The reason is simple: in being vulnerable, you
reach for your greatest need while risking your greatest pain. If
acceptance brings euphoria, then rejection brings shame and
heartbreak. By the time you reached adulthood, you likely had
enough painful experiences with rejection that risking your
heart was a serious struggle and one to avoid at all costs.

The lie that you are inherently unworthy to be loved may have
convinced you that hiding was your only option. And because
you're hiding, you want your spouse to hide too. You can't
handle the truth of who they are any more than you can handle
the truth of who you are. If you were dropped into the Garden
of Eden naked and saw other people running around naked, it
probably wouldn't feel like paradise at all. You would freak out
and want everyone to cover up as quickly as possible because
you cannot handle the idea of being exposed.

*God, it is scary to risk being rejected. Being vulnerable with our
needs could lead us to more pain. We trust You to take care of
our hearts, and to be with us when we feel the sting of rejection.*

Do you feel worthy of love? How can you come out of hiding?

FREE BENEFITS

Don't you realize that friendship with the world
makes you an enemy of God?

JAMES 4:4 NLT

Fear of rejection and shame sets you up to fall for the enemy's
counterfeits. Ever since sin entered the world and humanity
became disconnected from God, we have been looking for ways
to get our needs met outside of relationship or any scenario
where we are required to be vulnerable and risk our hearts.

You or your spouse may have always desperately sought the
benefits of intimacy without wanting to pay the price. The
enemy continues to offer the euphoric experiences you think
you can control—things like alcohol, drugs, sex, internet
pornography, shopping, carbohydrates, adrenaline, or cash.
You may use these things to give yourself a euphoric release
and take care of your needs, but you will have recognized that
none of those truly satisfy you.

*God, we know that nothing satisfies like You do. We don't
want to settle for counterfeit ways to meet our needs. Help us
to choose intimacy even though there is a cost. We know the
reward is well worth it.*

What is the benefit of intimacy?

Counterfeits

"If you were to give your allegiance to the world, they would love and welcome you as one of their own. But because you won't align yourselves with the values of this world, they will hate you. I have chosen you and taken you out of the world to be mine."

JOHN 15:19 TPT

Counterfeits always have ugly repercussions. Drunk drivers kill innocent people, young kids destroy their brains, men ignore the beautiful real women beside them in favor of images, people overspend and find themselves in serious debt, indulgent individuals eat themselves into morbid obesity and the host of diseases that accompany it, thrill seekers slowly become numb to reality, and selfish jerks don't care who they step on to get what they want.

Counterfeits never come through and they never satisfy. They are the perpetual carrot in front of the horse's nose, promising love, but it's always out of reach.

God, thank You that we can find our satisfaction in You. We confess that we look to counterfeit things to fill us with the love we need, but they are empty. They do us no good. Give us the strength to choose You and each other in the moments we feel most vulnerable.

What counterfeits tend to trip you up?

A Free Choice

For freedom Christ has set us free;
stand firm therefore, and do not submit again
to a yoke of slavery.

GALATIANS 5:1 ESV

Whenever you try to get your needs met through control, you end up being controlled and addicted. You lose your freedom. You enter into bondage that prevents the pain you are trying to self-medicate from ever being healed.

You and your spouse were made to have your needs met through relationships with people you don't control. Love—a free choice—is the only thing that will satisfy your hearts. This is why the counterfeits never live up to their promises. You must both face your fear of rejection, be healed of shame, and risk your hearts in your relationship. You have to be willing to offer the truth of who you are to each other and receive the truth from each other. Only the truth can make you free.

Jesus, we come to You today in need of healing. We have been hurt and rejected, and we live with shame that You don't want us to carry. Help us to share the truth with each other and find freedom in Your love.

What truths do you need to share with each other?

SCRATCH THE ITCH

We also pray that you will be strengthened with all his glorious power so you will have all the endurance and patience you need.

COLOSSIANS 1:11 NLT

The trust cycle model helps you build trust when you communicate with each other. The deepest part of your relational connection is getting to the need that you each have. It's like scratching your spouse's back and trying to find the exact place that itches, but you can't find it because you can't feel it. It's pretty dissatisfying for both parties when someone can't find that itchy spot.

The same could be said about discovering each other's needs. If you don't know what or where they are, you won't be able to satisfy the need. How will you help each other find those needs? You need to communicate a specific target that your spouse can hit to increase your relational satisfaction.

God, help us to communicate what we need to each other. It's not always easy to figure it out, so give us the patience to stick with it until we get to the bottom of it.

How well do you communicate where the itch is?

CREATING A LOOP

"How could a loving mother forget her nursing child
and not deeply love the one she bore?
Even if there is a mother who forgets her child,
I could never, no never, forget you."

ISAIAH 49:15 TPT

Imagine you have a little baby. Babies learn to communicate with their mother and father through need. They cry, and you try to figure out what they need and how you can help them. As soon as the baby expresses that they have a need, you go to action. The need being expressed has led to a response that says, "I care about what you need. Let me see if I can meet that need."

When the need is met, the child is satisfied. Whatever it is—the anxiety or discomfort—is gone and the baby is comfortable. You have just created a loop that leads to a bond. The bond forms because the baby expressed what was needed, there was a response to that need, and the baby was made comfortable.

Father, from the beginning of life, we were created to express our needs and have them met. Help us to practice this with each other, giving the patience and grace needed as we grow in our ability to meet the needs that are present.

How have you been creating loops in your relationship?

RESPONSE FROM HEAVEN

"I tell you the truth. It is to your advantage that I go away;
for if I do not go away, the Helper will not come to you;
but if I depart, I will send Him to you."

JOHN 16:7 NKJV

The role of the Holy Spirit in your life is to meet the deep needs
you express. Jesus said, "I have to go, but I will leave you with
the Comforter." As you learn to express what you need, there's
a response from heaven and your need is met. Then there is
ease and peace, and you feel more connected to God.

The bond, that connection process, begins to accelerate
between the two people who are relating to and with each
other. You express what you need, and your spouse responds.
They express what they need, and you respond. This is how you
build connection.

*God, thank You for sending the Holy Spirit to us as a comforter.
We are so grateful for the peace He offers when we express our
needs. Help us to work toward meeting each other's needs in a
way that creates connection and peace.*

When did you last ask the Holy Spirit to meet your needs?

MISTRUST CYCLE

Let's hold firmly to the confession of our hope without
wavering, for He who promised is faithful.

HEBREWS 10:23 NASB

There is another life cycle that happens when your needs
aren't met. This is how you build a mistrust cycle: one of you
communicates what you need, but there's no response so you
are left in your pain and anxiety. You may even be told to "just
deal with it."

If this happens continually in your marriage, you begin to pick
up that it's not safe to communicate your needs because they
either get neglected, or there is another poor reaction that
doesn't meet your need. This ongoing loop begins to destroy
trust. It attacks your bond and weakens your connection.

*Faithful God, thank You for Your goodness to us and Your
consistency in meeting our needs. You never break trust and
always know exactly what we need. Help us to learn how to
build trust with each other and not destroy it.*

*Can you identify any mistrust cycles in your relationship?
What can you do to eliminate those?*

A SPECIFIC SKILL

Do not be eager in your spirit to be angry,
For anger resides in the heart of fools.
ECCLESIASTES 7:9 NASB

To truly engage in an effective process of communication, you have to be able to get to the bottom of your needs. You both must figure out how to find, communicate, and listen for the need. This requires a specific skill set.

If you don't know what you need, or you don't know what you feel, you are not alone. A lot of people are in the same boat. You may think you can ignore what you need. You just shove it down and pretend you don't have any needs. But one day you'll wake up and find you suddenly "hate" your spouse. The reality is that you will have finally had the realization that you are in all kinds of pain in your relationship. This is avoidable. You must learn to find and communicate your needs.

God, we need Your help in finding and communicating our needs. We don't want to ignore that they are there and end up being in a resentful relationship. Give us wisdom as we search our hearts.

How can you develop the specific skill of finding and communicating your needs?

A REVELATION

A person without self-control
is like a city with broken-down walls.
PROVERBS 25:28 NLT

One of the most effective ways to communicate what's going on inside of you is through those I messages. Start with, "I feel…" You feel feelings; you don't feel thoughts. That's a revelation in itself. If you find yourself saying, "I feel like…" you should stop. That would be describing a thought. "I feel like you're a jerk." This doesn't describe what is going on inside of you. "I feel rejected, hurt, and lonely." Now you're getting somewhere.

An easy way to know if what you are about to express is a thought or feeling is to insert the word *think* in your sentence instead of *feel*. If it still makes sense, what you are about to say isn't a feeling. "I think you're a jerk." See, that's a thought not a feeling. "I think rejected, hurt, and lonely." That doesn't make sense because it is not a thought. Those are feelings. The better you get at communicating your feelings, the clearer the target you create for your spouse who cares about you and wants to satisfy your needs.

God, give us the self-control to speak to each other in ways that communicate our feelings and not just thoughts. Show us how to control our tongues.

How well do you distinguish the difference between thoughts and feelings?

RAINBOW OF EMOTIONS

A joyful heart is good medicine,
but a crushed spirit dries up the bones.
PROVERBS 17:22 ESV

The first step is to communicate what you are feeling. You are experiencing someone or something a certain way. This is vital information your spouse doesn't know. You or your spouse may often express that you feel angry. This might be the only feeling you have words for because you don't actually know your other feelings.

It could take a little time to figure out what is going on inside of you. You have a whole rainbow of emotions, but putting words to feelings may be a new concept for you. Children behave their feelings because they don't have words. If you don't figure out how you feel, you may find yourself acting like a child—kicking, slamming doors, yelling, or crying. Allow yourselves some time to discover your feelings, so you can better communicate with each other.

God, thank You for creating us with feelings. It's so easy to be confused about what we are feeling specifically, so we look to You to help us in our journey of discovering and communicating our many emotions.

How easy is it for you to identify and communicate your feelings?

FEELINGS CONNECTED

Create in me a clean heart, O God,
and renew a right spirit within me.
PSALM 51:10 ESV

When you feel something, connected to that feeling
is generally something that was said or done. In your
communication, you need to identify what happened and
connect it to the feeling. Help your spouse understand what it
is related to, and then say what you need to feel instead.

Telling your spouse you need to feel something is not the same
as telling them what you need them to do. For example, if you
say you feel hurt because your spouse didn't come home right
away last night, and you need them to come straight home
from work the next night, that isn't communicating what
you need to feel; it's trying to control your spouse. This will
just lead to more anxiety. Instead, you can express that when
your spouse doesn't come home, you need to feel something
different than what you felt the last time it happened.

*God, we want to make this relationship work. We want
connection and closeness. Help us figure out how to
communicate what we need to feel with each other.*

What do you most need to feel from each other?

GOOD INFORMATION

The tongue of the wise makes knowledge pleasant,
But the mouth of fools spouts foolishness.

PROVERBS 15:2 NASB

When you are trying to communicate feelings with each other, it can get out of hand pretty quickly. Remember to use feelings—not judgments, thoughts, or opinions—when you are expressing yourself. If you or your spouse begins throwing out judgments, your feelings will likely end up being invalidated or ignored. You have to pay attention to the feelings, so you don't continue damaging your relationship.

The first time that communication doesn't go well, you are a victim. After that, you have the choice to be powerful. Give your spouse good information about how you are feeling and what you need to feel instead. Both of you should communicate in a way that sends the message that you care. This will lower anxiety and minimize the experience of fear in your relationship.

God, we need Your wisdom both in sharing and listening. We trust You to help us communicate good information with each other that will help lower anxiety and build our connection.

How can you choose to be powerful in communicating your feelings?

CONNECTIVE CONVERSATIONS

The hearts of the wise make their mouths prudent,
and their lips promote instruction.

PROVERBS 16:23 NIV

There are a couple things you need from each other in your connective conversations. You need to hear from each other and feel valued when you talk. You each tell each other what is going on inside. This will lower anxiety because you are giving your spouse great information to work with, so they can make good decisions that help meet the need you have.

When you hit those conversations that have been troublesome in the past, instead of blowing past the good information you received from your spouse, you adjust because you understand what they need. Remember, the deepest level of communication is finding what your spouse needs and then meeting that need.

Father, You care about our deepest needs, and You meet them perfectly. We know we won't ever be as perfect at that as You are, but we want to try. When we learn what our spouse needs, help us to remember that need in future conversations, so we show our care for each other.

What makes you feel like you have truly connected in your conversations?

REINFORCED CONNECTION

There is only one kind of person who is worse than a fool:
the impetuous one who speaks without thinking first.

PROVERBS 29:20 TPT

As you begin to master the I message, be mindful of when you
may be sharing a thought instead of a feeling. Thoughts are
less vulnerable; when you describe them, it's about something
out there, not something inside you. When you feel sad, lonely,
rejected, or punished, you need to share those feelings and also
say what it is that you need to feel instead. Generally, what you
need to feel is the opposite: content, safe, understood, loved, etc.

When your goal is connection, it affects the tools you use to
communicate. When you feel love and connection, you need
to communicate these good feelings too. "I love when we're
together." "I like this experience." "I want more of this." Positive
communication that tells your spouse more about what you
enjoy is also good information that reinforces your connection.

*God, we know it takes time and practice to get this all right.
Give us patience and grace in the process of learning how to
best communicate our needs and our care for each other.*

*What positive communication can you share
with each other right now?*

WHAT'S AT STAKE

If you shrug off an insult and refuse to take offense,
you demonstrate discretion indeed.
But the fool has a short fuse
and will immediately let you know when he's offended.
PROVERBS 12:16 TPT

When you chose to walk together in a relationship, there was never a question of whether you would experience conflict. That was inevitable. The question is if you know what is at stake when conflict happens. The health of the relational connection is what you're risking.

Conflict is to a relationship what disease or injury is to a body. The goal in a relationship should be to prevent as much conflict as possible. However, in the same way that fighting off a disease or doing therapy after an injury can strengthen your body, passing through the flames of conflict in a healthy, productive way can strengthen a relational connection.

God, we admit that we thought it might be a little easier to live with each other than what we have experienced. Help us to pursue good connection in spite of conflict.

Do you experience more or less conflict in your relationship than what you had imagined?

A Positive Outcome

Let us consider how we may spur one another on toward love
and good deeds, not giving up meeting together, as some are in
the habit of doing, but encouraging one another—and all the
more as you see the Day approaching.

HEBREWS 10:24-25 NIV

It is possible to end up on the other side of conflict as more
powerful individuals, freer to be yourselves, more confident in
your love for each other, and more hopeful about your ability
to meet each other's needs.

This positive outcome to conflict is dependent, however, on
what you choose to do. Will you allow conflict to tear your
connection apart? Or will you fight for your connection in the
midst of conflict?

*Father, You are present even in our conflict. You don't run away
and leave us to figure everything out on our own. Holy Spirit,
help us to listen to Your gentle words of wisdom that calm a
situation down instead of stirring up further contention. Your
way is always the best way.*

What is your goal when you face conflict?

REVIEW THE GOALS

God is not unjust. He will not forget how hard you have
worked for him and how you have shown your love to him by
caring for other believers, as you still do.

HEBREWS 6:10 NLT

Take a moment with your spouse to review the communication
goals in a marriage relationship.

- Our first goal in a conversation is to understand one
  another.
- Both of our thoughts, feelings, and needs are valuable
  and important.
- We will not participate in disrespectful conversations.
  When thoughts, feelings, and needs are devalued in a
  conversation, we will stop the conversation and set a
  clear boundary. Until respect is restored, we will not
  participate.
- We will communicate our true feelings and needs to
  establish trust and intimacy.
- It is each person's job to say what is going on inside
  of them. We understand neither of us has powers of
  telepathy or the right to assume we know one another's
  motives, thoughts, feelings, or needs.

Take a breath and re-read that list. The rest of the goals will be
summarized tomorrow!

God, help us to choose to keep our love on.

Which of these goals are the most difficult for you to pursue?

SECOND SET

Do not forget to do good and to share with others,
for with such sacrifices God is pleased.

HEBREWS 13:16 NIV

Take a moment to review the second set of communication goals together.

- The best way to communicate our feelings and needs is to use I messages and clear, specific statements that show what we are feeling and experiencing.
- We will not expect each other to know our feelings and needs unless we have communicated them already.
- We will not make judgment statements or tell each other how to change in order to meet our needs.
- When needs are being communicated, we will listen well so we can understand the need, see how our lives are affecting each other, and do what we can to meet each other's needs.
- We are committed to protecting and nurturing our connection. We will keep moving toward each other— no matter what.
- We will manage our own hearts so we can respond in love and cast out fear.

Take a breath and re-read that list. There is great hope for closer connection when you pursue goals together.

God, we look to You to be our perfect guide.

Which of these goals do you pursue the best?

HEALTHY AND RESISTANT

Two are better than one,
because they have a good return for their labor:
If either of them falls down, one can help the other up.
But pity anyone who falls and has no one to help them up.
Also, if two lie down together, they will keep warm.
But how can one keep warm alone?
ECCLESIASTES 4:9-11 NIV

The core values and tools of communication you reviewed over the last two days will prevent most conflict in relationships. Every time you express your needs, set a boundary, listen, meet a need, or speak in one another's love language, you are nourishing and exercising your connection. This keeps it healthy and resistant to harm.

Healthy communication often feels like hard work. A vulnerable, honest conversation requires as much energy from your minds and hearts as a tough session at the gym requires of your body. But the benefits of building a strong connection are even more rewarding than the rewards of building a strong body. This is where the promise of the Scripture above comes into play.

Thank You for Your encouragement, God. We believe in Your Word that tells us it is better for us to be together than alone.

What can you do this week to nourish your relationship?

CORD STRENGTH

Though one may be overpowered, two can defend themselves.
A cord of three strands is not quickly broken.
ECCLESIASTES 4:12 NIV

How strong do you want your cord—your connection—to be? What level of difficulty do you want to prepare your relationship to withstand? What are some of the tests you may be required to face?

Answering these questions will help you stay focused and intentional as you keep your relationship in shape. Just like people who try to get lean and healthy have goal, you need to know what you are aiming for and regularly remind yourself of what's at stake in meeting your goal, so you can sustain your motivation.

God, we want to be prepared to face the challenges and trials that come our way in life. We know You are faithful to help us through each situation. You are the third strand in our cord. Make us strong with You.

Do you remember what you are aiming for in your relationship?

LAZY MOMENTS

Whatever you do, in word or deed,
do everything in the name of the Lord Jesus,
giving thanks to God the Father through him.

COLOSSIANS 3:17 ESV

It's so natural when things seem to be moving along well in a relationship to ease off the gas and coast. If you bought flowers for your wife yesterday and told her you love her, or you made your husband his favorite dinner, you think that should be good for a week.

Too many days like this is like eating too many donuts when you have a plan to be healthy. One day you get up and realize you are really far away from your goal. And in your relationship, that means you are far away from each other. What happened? You got lazy, that's all. Though it may not hurt you today, someday soon a conflict will pull on your cord of connection, and you're going to want it to be strong.

Father, help us not to be lazy in our pursuit of a healthy marriage. We want to keep putting in the effort required to meet our goals and become closer.

Have you recognized those lazy moments in your relationship?

DURING THE CALM

He calms the storm,
So that its waves are still.
PSALM 107:29 NKJV

Don't back off from brave communication strength training. If you can pass the test of prioritizing your connection when seas are calm, then you'll be ready to pass that test in the storm.

Just like athletes practice outside of competitions, soldiers train during times of peace, and emergency personnel run drills to prepare for real crises, you can develop good habits of communication while storms aren't visible, so you are prepared when they do appear. Then you won't have to worry about your cord becoming so fragile that it breaks under the slightest pressure.

God, help us to develop the skills we need in our relationship to communicate well when conflict comes. You are the peace in every storm, and we rely on You to see us through each one.

How can you prioritize your connection this week?

TESTED CONNECTIONS

"The one who eats My flesh and drinks My blood has eternal
life, and I will raise him up on the last day."

JOHN 6:54 NASB

Jesus communicated in ways that intentionally tested His
connections with people. He confronted people with truth that
He knew they would probably reject. His deeply controversial
statement about eating His flesh was enough to get an entire
crowd to walk away from their connection with Him. Only
the twelve stuck around. When asked if they were going to
disconnect too, the disciples responded honestly. It had crossed
their minds, but they knew there was nowhere else to go that
offered them true life.

The disciples held on to their connection with Jesus even
though they had as many theological and intellectual
disagreements with His outrageous words as every other Jew
who heard them. The true significance of Jesus' words was not
unveiled until after His death and resurrection. Despite this
and many other mysteries Jesus threw at His disciples, they
stayed with Him.

*Jesus, thank You for showing us that sticking with our most
important relationships and the connections we have in them
is worth it. We trust that You want what is best for us.*

*What significance is there in sticking with
your marriage relationship?*

HOLD ON

When many of his disciples heard it, they said,
"This is a hard saying; who can listen to it?"
After this, many of his disciples turned back
and no longer walked with him.

JOHN 6:60, 66 ESV

Jesus purposely created opportunities for His followers to prioritize their connection above offense, confusion, or disagreement. He knew they needed practice if they were going to protect their connection to the end. Connection with Him was more important than being right. He taught them how to hold on to the most powerful Person in the universe no matter what, and as a result, they turned the world upside down.

Learning to pass the test of connection in the midst of conflict can make you and your spouse more powerful as individuals and give you a stronger connection than you could have ever imagined.

God, when we prioritize our connection with You, it has a positive effect on our connection with each other. In times of testing, help us to look to You when we feel offended or confused. We want to respond well to the test and create a stronger connection with each other.

How can you change the way you view conflict in your marriage?

MAJOR ADJUSTMENTS

He who does not love does not know God, for God is love.
1 JOHN 4:8 NKJV

Perhaps you married someone who is exactly like you with the exact same needs. Maybe expressing your needs and getting them met comes naturally for both of you. *Or not.* You and your spouse may fall at opposite ends of the spectrum when it comes to personality and temperament. Your needs could be very different.

Communicating and meeting your needs will likely require major adjustments and growth in both of you. Be encouraged! When you develop the art of responding to one another's needs in love rather than reacting in fear, you will build a connection that is strong enough to face any potential conflict. You can go from being relational pudgy weaklings to champion bodybuilders. It may take some time, but when you put in the effort and keep your love on, you could find yourselves in a relationship where nothing has the power to break you apart.

Father, thank You for creating us all so differently. You know what it will take to make our bond so strong that it is difficult to break it apart. Give us the patience to endure as we adjust and grow.

What adjustments have you had to make to strengthen your bond?

WE NEED TO TALK

You, Lord, are forgiving and good,
abounding in love to all who call to you.
PSALM 86:5 NIV

Conflict can become dangerously ugly when you and your spouse react out of fear and pain. Fear feeds conflict because it is, at its core, opposed to connection. When you can recognize what happens when your natural defenses are triggered by a perceived threat, you can put a plan of action in place to get fear under control and minimize the damage to your connection.

Imagine someone you know approaches you out of the blue and says, "Hey, we need to talk." Are you hit with racing thoughts and a rapid heartbeat? Do you get angry? Do you stay out of sight, try to weasel your way out of the conversation, make excuses, or dance around the issue? Or do you just shut down? All of these are classic fear reactions—fight, flight, or freeze—and all will damage your connection if you let them.

God, we know that this life is fraught with conflict. Why do we think we can avoid it? Why does it make us so uncomfortable? Help us to lean in to learning and developing our relationship as we walk through difficult seasons.

*How do you feel when someone says they need to talk?
Why do you think you have that reaction?*

CLASSIC REACTION

Beloved, let's love one another; for love is from God, and everyone who loves has been born of God and knows God.

1 JOHN 4:7 NASB

What is your classic fear reaction? If you or your spouse have a fight response to fear, a verbal spat can turn into drag-out mortal combat, which is obviously damaging. But it's just as ugly if you have the flight response. This would look like running away, telling lies, and pretending everything is all right. A freeze responder will simply refuse to engage and turn off their love. It may not look violent, but when you look at how it poisons and starves the life out of a connection, it is definitely ugly.

Because fear is so prevalent in the human race, it is likely that you have found yourselves responding in one of these three harmful ways. But there is hope! Remember, perfect love casts out fear, and as you work to eliminate fear from your relationship, you will build your connection.

God, we do not want to respond in fear to each other in our moments of conflict. Help us to identify our fear reactions and begin to work on expelling fear from our relationship.

What is your natural response to conflict?

RED BUTTON

If possible, so far as it depends on you,
live peaceably with all.
ROMANS 12:18 ESV

If you want to avoid ugly, you must have a plan for how you are going to respond when your spouse pushes that giant red button on your chest and invites you into a duel. There is a real chance they are already under the influence of fear, pain, and anger, and they may not be ready to manage themselves well in the conversation.

This should be expected. Scared, hurting people do not usually play fair. They might even come across as being mean. You may have watched in shock as fear turned your normally kind and calm spouse into a seemingly treacherous, spiteful, or even violent person. But that is what the spirit of fear does—it brings out the worst in people. You must create a plan for responding without fear.

God of peace, in You there is no fear. Help us to walk in the assurance of Your love and care, and to avoid letting fear creep into our responses.

What is your plan for responding to conflict?

DUELING SWORD

Be cheerful! Repair whatever is broken among you, as your hearts are being knit together in perfect unity. Live continually in peace, and God, the source of love and peace, will mingle with you.

2 CORINTHIANS 13:11 TPT

If you want to protect your connection, then you need to learn to defuse fear bombs and constantly steer would-be duels into respectful conversations. Only a respectful conversation is going to be productive in resolving a conflict.

Both of you have equal responsibility in setting your own boundaries for how many disrespectful, unproductive, or damaging exchanges you will endure. The moment either of you picks up the dueling sword, you are equally guilty for whatever blood is shed.

God, we desire to protect our relationship. We want to eliminate fear and anxiety from our connection. Give us the grace and strength we need to keep our conversations respectful when we are dealing with conflict.

How do you steer conversations toward respect?

RESPECTFUL CONVERSATION

If I were to speak with eloquence in earth's many languages,
and in the heavenly tongues of angels, yet I didn't express
myself with love, my words would be reduced to the hollow
sound of nothing more than a clanging symbol.

1 CORINTHIANS 13:1 TPT

A respectful conversation has a goal, and it has a process for
achieving that goal. If either of you refuse to agree to the goal
and won't engage in the process, the conversation will fail in
the respectful category.

The goal of a respectful conversation is to strengthen your
relational connection by discovering what you or your spouse
needs and learning how to meet that need. If either or you are
hurt or afraid, it can be tricky to ascertain the need. Often, the
first issue you need to confront is your spouse's belief that you
do not care about their needs. This must be exposed and dealt
with; otherwise, instead of communicating a problem, your
spouse will try to communicate a solution, and that is destined
for failure. Your spouse needs to know that you do in fact care
about their needs.

*Father, You care so deeply about each of us, and You know what
we need to do to communicate care and respect through conflict.
Show us how to honor each other as we work toward a goal of
greater connection.*

What is your respectful conversation goal?

VULNERABILITY FOR RESOLUTION

Turn away from evil and do good.
Search for peace, and work to maintain it.
1 PETER 3:11 NLT

It's pretty impossible to create a solution to a problem if you don't know what the problem is. And you're not going to identify the problem unless you are willing to admit what you need and trust each other to care about that need when you show it.

This is where you must confront your deepest fears of vulnerability and rejection. Trying to convince your spouse to care about your needs without being vulnerable enough to communicate them is an exercise in futility, yet so many people fall into this fear-driven pattern. It's not easy, but true conflict resolution—the kind that heals and strengthens a relational connection—will not be achieved without it.

God, in spite of fears that have plagued us in the past, we want to move forward in our ability to be vulnerable with each other and trust that we mutually care. We need healing in our connection, and we know that is possible with You.

How good are you at being vulnerable about your needs?

THE REAL PROBLEM

The name of the LORD is a fortified tower;
the righteous run to it and are safe.

PROVERBS 18:10 NIV

Perhaps one of you has been feeling disconnected and unloved
for a while. Your spouse may suspect something is wrong and
might even ask you. Because you don't feel cared for, you may
lash out with accusations of neglect. "You don't care." "You
don't listen." "You're never home." "You don't understand." You
might even question if your spouse still loves you. And when
they assure you that they do, you'll likely tell them they only
said it because you told them to.

You will never find a resolution when communication looks
like that. You are afraid because your needs aren't getting
met, but they aren't getting met because you are afraid to
communicate them. When you get your spouse to act by
coercion, it won't meet your need because your real need can
only be met by a free act of love. To show your spouse the real
problem, you must overcome your fear, trust that they care,
and tell them what you need.

*God, give us eyes to see when our spouse is hurting, and give us
ears to truly listen to their need without responding in fear.*

*Can you identify with this situation?
What do you think is the real problem?*

CLEAR MESSAGES

Agree to live in unity with one another and put to rest any division that attempts to tear you apart. Be restored as one united body living in perfect harmony. Form a consistent choreography among yourselves, having a common perspective with shared values.

1 CORINTHIANS 1:10 TPT

Communicating the message that you care about your spouse's needs at the beginning of a respectful conversation is crucial. The next step is discovering what the need is through the process of sending and receiving clear messages to one another.

In order for this process to be successful, you must have both a speaker and a listener. If either component is missing, you either have silence or a collective monologue. Neither of these constitutes a conversation.

Father, we believe that with Your help we can communicate both our care and our willingness to listen to each other. Give us patience in this process of discovering and sharing our needs.

Which non-conversation do you find happens most often in your relationship: silence or collective monologue? How can you change this?

ONE ROLE AT A TIME

Live peacefully with each other.
1 Thessalonians 5:13 NLT

Imagine that you have a beautiful 60-inch, flat-screen television and a top-of-the-line Blu-ray disc player. In order for this entertainment system to work, you need all the correct cables plugged into the right spots. When you put your favorite movie in the Blu-ray player, it will read its contents and send the information through the cables to the TV. The TV will then interpret that information and turn it into images.

In a respectful conversation, one of you is the Blu-ray player and the other is the TV. It's very important that you only play one of these roles at a time, or you will end up with a processing error. If you are the Blu-ray player, your job is to read the contents of your thoughts, feelings, and needs, and send a clear message about those contents to the TV. The TV's job is to receive the message and display it back to you. Only when you both agree that the message has been successfully communicated and understood can you switch roles or begin to discuss solutions.

God, we understand that in order to have a respectful conversation, we need to take turns talking and listening. Help us to work on our processing systems and cables as we develop closeness.

Which role do you find most difficult to play?

JUMBLED CODE

The LORD will give strength to His people;
The LORD will bless His people with peace.
PSALM 29:11 NASB

Because you are humans, and not machines, sending and
receiving messages is a little more dynamic and will take more
time and effort. As the message sender, you might struggle to
read what is going on inside you, especially if you are dealing
with fear and don't have a lot of practice identifying your
needs. You will probably throw out a bunch of messages that
are still in some kind of jumbled code.

The receiver of the message needs to help the sender decipher
the code by asking questions: "Is this what you're saying? Is
this how you are feeling?" None of these should be asked or
interpreted as judgments but as honest attempts to clarify what
has been said. As the receiver feeds back the sender's message,
the sender should identify discrepancies and make corrections:
"No, that's not what I was trying to say. Let me try this again. I
actually feel..."

*Thank You, Father, for perfectly interpreting the jumbled code we
send so often. We can love each other because You first loved us.*

*How can you better decipher the jumbled code of
what your spouse needs?*

No Conversation

Be like-minded, be sympathetic, love one another,
be compassionate and humble.
1 Peter 3:8 niv

As the message sender, it's your responsibility to stick to
reading your needs and not offering your opinions and
judgments of the listener. Connection cables are in danger
of shorting out when accusations begin flying. If you're the
receiver of a "you" attack, you might try to give your spouse a
pass and see if they are willing to reframe their you message as
an I message. If they cannot, you need to set a boundary and
offer to continue the conversation when your spouse is ready to
show their heart instead of telling you what's wrong with you.

Every respectful conversation needs one speaker and one
listener at all times. Two Blu-ray players cannot communicate
with one another. They will never know what movies they are
trying to play until they hook up with a TV. No one listening
means there is no more conversation.

*God, this communication thing can be tricky! Help us to always
be ready to listen to each other's needs and to set boundaries
when conversations become disrespectful.*

Have you chosen to have respectful conversations lately?

TRUE SERVANT ROLE

In your relationships with one another,
have the same mindset as Christ Jesus:
Who, being in very nature God, did not consider equality with
God something to be used to his own advantage; rather, he
made himself nothing by taking the very nature of a servant,
being made in human likeness.

PHILIPPIANS 2:5-7 NIV

Though it does require humility and vulnerability for the
message sender to show the receiver what is going on inside,
listening is the true servant role in a respectful conversation.
The listener affirms that the conversation is about the message
sender and their needs, but in the end, the listener is really
the winner. If you listen well, you will have two vital pieces of
information—what your spouse needs and what you need to do.

With those two pieces of information, you can start to identify
and take ownership of the problem and create an effective
solution. If you become a skilled listener, you will begin to
more easily identify what your spouse truly needs and take
ownership for meeting that need.

*Jesus, thank You for Your real-life example of servanthood.
We desire to be more like You in all ways including our ability
to listen and serve. Teach us specifically what that looks like
in our marriage.*

*What needs have you heard lately that you
can take ownership for meeting?*

Skilled Listeners

Catch all the foxes,
those little foxed,
before they ruin the vineyard of love,
for the grapevines are blossoming!
SONG OF SOLOMON 2:15 NLT

A skilled listener with a servant's heart is the deadliest weapon against the fear-bombs that threaten connection. When you get two skilled listeners working together, watch out! You and your spouse could become ninjas at keeping fear away from your connection. As you engage in the mutual dance of going low and serving one another, you are going to remove all doubt that you care for each other.

You can then operate with the assumption that you both care about each other's needs. You invite and offer the exchange of truth every day in your relationship, and you stay connected. The more connection becomes the normal state of your relationship, the more quickly you will recognize signs of disconnection and be able to nip them—and their potentially deadly side effects—in the bud.

God, help us to work toward removing doubt and fear from our relationship. Keep us aware of the little foxes that create big issues in our connection and show us how to chase them away.

What can you do to become skilled listeners with servant hearts?

THE MOMENTUM

He who says he abides in Him
ought himself also to walk just as He walked.

1 JOHN 2:6 NKJV

Most problems are solved in the momentum of protecting connection. But even when connecting does not solve a problem, it helps to keep the problem under control. Maybe you have strongly opposing ideas about a certain topic. You could be like two freight trains moving in opposite directions. You may have argued intensely and concluded that the disagreement was going to injure your relationship. In this case, you must choose to protect your relationship.

You may disagree strongly about something very important to both of you, but together you keep elevating your relationship above that issue in your hearts and minds. This affects how you treat each other, how you talk about one another, and how you talk to each other. Refuse to let your disagreement move you away from each other. If you can prioritize connection in the midst of conflict, you are going to have something even more powerful to hold onto down the road.

God, we want to be moving in the same direction—with each other and toward each other. When we disagree on things that are important to each of us, help us to prioritize our connection.

Have you had to agree to disagree on an issue? How can you continue to strengthen your connection around the issue?

FITNESS PLAN

Above all, you must live as citizens of heaven, conducting yourselves in a manner worthy of the Good News about Christ. Then, whether I come see you again or only hear about you, I will know that you are standing together with one spirit and one purpose, fighting together for the faith, which is the Good News.

PHILIPPIANS 1:27 NLT

Get started on your relational connection fitness plan. Get off the couch and strengthen the cords of connection. Start respectful conversations by clarifying that you care deeply about each other's needs. Send and receive clear messages. Don't participate in conversations if both of you don't want to be respectful.

Choose to keep your love on, nuke fear, believe the best about each other, and trust that you both care. If at times you don't care, repent, turn your love back on, and forgive each other. Move toward your spouse even when it hurts.

Father, You don't give up on us even when we run away from You and make terrible decisions. You are always loving and always good. You forgive us and welcome us back into our connection with You. We want to do the same for each other.

What is your relational connection fitness plan?

CHOOSING A GOAL

You formed my inward parts;
you knitted me together in my mother's womb.

PSALM 139:13 ESV

Conflict happens when you have a relationship with another human being. In your marriage relationship, there's an excellent chance for disagreement because something will happen that hurts or is disappointing. Learn to communicate through conflict successfully and gain a strong relationship as a result.

It all starts with the goal you choose. If agreement is your goal, meaning you need your spouse to agree with you before you can move on, you set yourself up for disconnection and ongoing arguments. You also communicate that your spouse can't be themselves around you; they have to be *you* around you. When you make the goal understanding instead, you listen for needs that are different than what you have, and you choose a communication style that lowers anxiety.

Thank You, God, that we are fully known and understood by You. You allow us to be ourselves even though that means we are flawed and imperfect. Help us to listen for needs that are different than our own and to make understanding our goal in communication.

Is your communication goal agreement or understanding?

CONNECTION STRENGTH

Wait for the LORD;
be strong, and let your heart take courage;
wait for the LORD!
PSALM 27:14 ESV

Remember that aggressive, passive, and passive-aggressive communication styles all juice up anxiety, are rooted in fear, and attempt to control others. Assertive communicators send the message that both parties in the relationship matter. There can be two powerful people in your conversations. The key is to focus on the connection and to prioritize that connection in conflict.

The quality of your relationship is at stake as you discuss whatever it is that you disagree on. In order to have a successful conflict, you have to measure the strength of your connection. If you have a fragile connection, you're not going to be able to sort out a giant problem. You won't have much influence with each other. The goal is to build the connection, protect it, and develop it so you can work on big disagreements as well as protect your connection.

God, we know we aren't going to agree on everything all the time. You have created us as individuals, and we both want to be powerful in our relationship. Help us protect our connection as we work on resolving conflicts.

What is the strength of your connection today?

HANDLE WITH CARE

The mind of the discerning acquires knowledge,
And the ear of the wise seeks knowledge.

PROVERBS 18:15 NASB

What is the strength of your connection? If you and your spouse disagree over where to eat or what movie to watch, you could find yourselves disconnected more quickly than you'd like. Your connection could be so fragile that it breaks over those small choices. You typically end up in that situation because the quality of your relationship hasn't been something you've worked on.

You may need to tend to the reality that you are quite different. Perhaps you've never really listened, or adjusted, or served. Maybe you haven't wanted to work on the connection because it has always been so weak. Spend some time working on your connection and it will become stronger.

God, our connection needs work. It needs strengthening. Help us to commit to prioritizing building our connection and moving toward each other.

Does disconnection happen in your relationship over seemingly unimportant issues?

REAL CONVERSATIONS

A fool is in love with his own opinion,
but wisdom means being teachable.
PROVERBS 12:15 TPT

When you have been working on your connection and you
hit a point of disagreement or conflict, you can have an actual
conversation about it. You recognize your spouse really needs
you to listen, to stay connected, and to move from where you
were to where both of you are now. You might not feel like
moving, but it's your desire to protect the connection that
moves you together.

When you pay close attention to the strength of your
connection, it allows you to put a bigger load on your
relationship. Real conversations about sex, money, children,
and in-laws are possible. You can share your needs freely, and
you know your spouse will behave differently in an effort to
serve your need. Of course, it isn't foolproof. Occasionally,
even if your connection is really strong, something can
sideswipe you. When you feel a disconnect, try to reconnect as
quickly as possible.

*God, we ask that You would continue to help us strengthen our
connection. We want to be able to share openly and honestly
with each other even when topics are troublesome.*

How often can you have real conversations with each other?

BAD TIMING

Look carefully then how you walk, not as unwise but as wise, making the best use of the time, because the days are evil.

EPHESIANS 5:15-16 ESV

When you're disconnected, it is not a good time to try to work out a problem. Disconnection typically means some level of fear is present. When you try to sort through a problem in that environment, your disconnection causes you to feel like you both care more about yourselves than you do about each other. You will know by now that when the two of you are afraid of each other, you will try to control each other, attempting to produce what you think you need without protecting your connection. You can't protect what you don't have.

When you're disconnected and there's an issue, take your relationship and put it above the issue. When you make finances, children, or any other issue more important than your connection, you are serving the issue instead of serving each other.

Father, thank You for giving us access to Your wisdom and guidance. We want to follow Your lead and work on our issues when the timing is right.

How good is your timing when it comes to discussing issues?

ADJUST AND SERVE

Pride leads to disgrace,
but with humility comes wisdom.
PROVERBS 11:2 NLT

How can you begin working on your connection? Start with
the love languages: learn them and learn how to best apply
them for your spouse. Move toward each other. Listen with
a desire to really hear what your spouse is saying. Send the
message that you love and care for each other. When you get
your connection back, anxiety will be gone, and you will both
feel heard. You will walk into conflicts ready to serve each
other, to adjust.

Keep conversations respectful by expecting to receive good
information you didn't already have and anticipate meeting
a need. You will be ready to change the way you've been
handling yourself. In that place of humility and honor, you will
communicate that your spouse is more valuable to you than
the checkbook, or your free time, or how you handle a stressful
situation. This is only possible when there is willingness to
adjust and serve.

*Thank You, God, for the value You place on us. You wanted
relationship with us so badly that You allowed Your Son to die
so we could be considered worthy. Help us remember Your gift
as we learn to serve each other.*

What do you expect in your respectful conversations?

KIND OF SUCCESS

The LORD gives wisdom;
from his mouth come knowledge and understanding.
PROVERBS 2:6 NIV

You might find yourself in situations where you both feel like what you did was acceptable or reasonable. This doesn't mean that you can't have a respectful conversation or shouldn't apologize if what happened is negatively affecting your connection. Sometimes all you need to do to break down the walls is to admit whatever part you played in the conflict and reiterate the love and value you have for your spouse and your relationship. This is not the same as agreement.

When you and your spouse can get to a place where you recognize your communication weaknesses and set your goal for closer connection, you can work through conflict and find peace. You listen and validate each other, and you build intimacy and trust through sharing. It's good to communicate with your spouse that this relationship is important to you, and that you want to build on it together.

God, success in Your kingdom is not measured the way it is in this world. Success to You looks like thriving relationships especially with the people closest to us. Help us to keep the right view of success in front of us.

Is working through conflict in a healthy way creating better connection for you?

WALKING IN THE LIGHT

If we walk in the light, as he is in the light,
we have fellowship with one another,
and the blood of Jesus his Son cleanses us from all sin.

1 JOHN 1:7 ESV

In a confrontation, you or your spouse may get hurt. Maybe both of you do. You can choose to stuff those feelings and let them fester, or you can bring them to the light. This can be a big challenge: to live in the light together.

When you live in the light, it brings things out of darkness and shows that you are willing to trust each other and put demands on the relationship so adjustments can be made, and needs can be met. Ultimately, you want comfort and peace in your relationship so the bond of trust can be built. If your conflict ends in greater connection, then it was a successful confrontation. This only happens when you purposefully protect the bond of your relationship.

Father, help us to walk in the light with You. We want to have fellowship with You and with each other. Give us the boldness to share our feelings and not let them fester in darkness.

Are you letting bad feelings fester?

HEALTHY BOUNDARIES

My son, share your love with your wife alone.
Drink from her well of pleasure and from no other.
PROVERBS 5:15 TPT

If you and your spouse walk through life without healthy boundaries, you are on the road that will destroy your relationship. You won't just harm your relationship with each other, you can do damage to all of your relationships. It is important to learn how to establish and protect appropriate boundaries in your lives.

You are both responsible to manage different levels of intimacy, responsibility, influence, and trust with people in your life. You are also responsible to honor the different levels of access and influence others allow you to have in their lives. These levels are absolutely righteous, healthy, normal, and good. When we expect that we should all have equal access to one another, we are setting ourselves up to violate and be violated.

God, we understand the need for boundaries in our lives. Give us wisdom in how and where we should set the boundaries and teach us to accept boundaries others have for us.

Are you good at setting boundaries?

PANIC ATTACK

Don't visit your neighbors too often,
or you will wear out your welcome.

PROVERBS 25:17 NLT

When you don't set boundaries around the levels of access and
intimacy with people in your life, you can quickly become a
target. When you agree to do things because you don't want
to upset your spouse or others in your life, you create an
environment that puts you moments away from losing your cool.

You might let the dog sleep in your bed even though that
keeps you awake, or allow someone to stay at your house for
too long, or lend money to someone who promises to pay you
back even though you can't really afford it. Contrary to popular
belief, these acts of kindness do not define a good Christian
life. These are prerequisites for a panic attack!

*God, You want us to be loving, kind, and generous. Sometimes
this makes me feel like I have to do everything for everyone. But
that is not what You demonstrated. You had healthy boundaries
that created an environment of love and peace.*

*How do you maintain a balance between
saying no and giving of yourself?*

PATTERN FOR LIFE

"Why did you seek Me?
Did you not know that I
must be about My Father's business?"
LUKE 2:49 NKJV

To see the pattern for the Christian life, look at Jesus. When you do, you will see that He prioritized certain relationships over others. He did not offer the same level of access and intimacy to everyone. His primary allegiance was always to the Father. At twelve years old, He was already about His Father's business. Everything Jesus did revolved around prioritizing that core relationship above all others.

After the Father, the Gospels indicate that Jesus' closest relationships were with the twelve disciples. These were the people He partnered with, traveled with, taught, trained, and trusted. Within that group, He was especially close to Peter, James, and John. They were privileged to share incredible revelations, encounters, and conversations with Jesus that no one else did. And of those three, we know that John was the one Jesus loved, the one He charged with taking over His role as Mary's son.

Jesus, thank You for showing us that our relationships don't all have to look the same. We were designed to be closer to some people than others. Help us to prioritize our relationship with You first, and then with each other.

Can you see the different intimacy levels in your life?

INNERMOST CIRCLE

The LORD is my chosen portion and my cup;
you hold my lot.
PSALM 16:5 ESV

Twelve. Three. One. This is the picture Jesus gave of how many relationships we humans have the capacity to cultivate, and how to prioritize them according to levels of intimacy. Cultivating and protecting levels of intimacy occurs best with boundaries.

Your innermost circle of intimacy is your core. You might call it your God Spot because He is the only person who belongs there—at the core of your heart and spirit. Nobody else knows you and loves you like Jesus, nobody else deserves your heart's primary allegiance and worship, and nobody should hold the place of influence He holds in your life.

God, we want You to take Your rightful place in our hearts. Help us to prioritize our time with You. You know us on a level that no one else does, and You love us completely.

How do you prioritize your relationship with God?

DEEPEST SOUL TIE

Let marriage be held in honor among all,
and let the marriage bed be undefiled.
HEBREWS 13:4 ESV

The next level of intimacy is for your most intimate human relationship, your deepest soul tie. Only one person is going to fit into that spot. If you are married, this should be your spouse. Prior to being married, someone else probably occupied your innermost circle of intimacy. You may have to face a delicate transition as you move the person who has been on that level back a spot or two and let your spouse take their place. It might be uncomfortable, but it must be done.

Once you get married, you can't let anyone else be more important to you. If you do, you are effectively putting your spouse in submission to that person, and that will not work out very well.

God, help us to reserve our most intimate human relationship for each other. We want to honor our marriage and prioritize each other, creating a deeper connection than we have with anyone else on earth.

How can you make your marriage relationship your most intimate human relationship if you haven't already?

OUTER CIRCLES

"This is my commandment:
Love each other in the same way I have loved you."
JOHN 15:12 NLT

The further out you go in the circles of intimacy, the more people you can fit in them. After your most intimate human relationship circle, the next circle contains people like children and grandchildren, followed by your closest friends and family members. Heading out further, you have good friends, then co-workers, and then acquaintances. Keep going and you find people in the same geographic location, and finally the rest of the human race.

Yes, you are called to love all people, but that doesn't mean that all people have access to your core. You may be called to pray for someone in Hollywood or even a group of terrorists. Praying for them does not mean that you will allow them into your core circle. It's your job to manage your life so you can offer the people in your inmost circles appropriate access to your core.

God, thank You for designing us with different levels of intimacy. You know what is good for us emotionally, physically, and spiritually. Help us to be mindful of the access we allow to the many people we are called to love.

Who do you see in each of your intimacy circles?

MOVED OUT

In all this you greatly rejoice, though now for a little while you may have had to suffer grief in all kinds of trials. These have come so that the proven genuineness of your faith—of greater worth than gold, which perishes even though refined by fire— may result in praise, glory and honor when Jesus Christ is revealed.

1 PETER 1:6-7 NIV

Sadly, sometimes people in your inner circle scare or hurt you very seriously. If they are unwilling to clean up the mess they made, you must move them out to a place of access that they can handle and that you are comfortable with.

Some people who once held an intimate place in your life may find themselves out in the "stranger" sphere after they break significant trust. You can choose to keep your love on toward them, but it may be a very long time (if ever) before you have them over for dinner.

God, we have been hurt by people in our lives who we used to feel very close to. Help us to exercise the right amount of caution in inviting them back in. We want to be loving, but we know we also need to be wise.

Is there someone who needs to be moved to a different circle of intimacy in your lives?

LEVEL OF ATTENTION

A friend is always loyal,
and a brother is born to help in time of need.
PROVERBS 17:17 NLT

The level of intimacy people have in your life determines how much of yourself you can offer when they pull on the relationship. If you are chatting with someone from church for the first time and they tell you the engine in their car blew up, you may give your sympathy and offer to pray for provision. If that person is a little closer, you may give them the number of your mechanic. Someone closer still, like a good friend, may be deserving of borrowing your car until theirs is fixed (if you can spare it).

Perhaps a child or other close family member would be worthy of you pulling out your wallet to cover some of the expenses. But if the person whose engine blew up is your spouse, there should be no doubt in your mind that you are about to purchase a new car. Your most intimate human relationship deserves all your time, money, energy, and resources that will help bring a solution to the problem at hand.

Father, sometimes we get confused about how much help we should offer in situations. Helping seems like the right thing to do, but we recognize that the level of help we offer should depend on the closeness of relationship.

*Does your level of attention match
your relationship intimacy level?*

DO NOT DISTURB

Contribute to the needs of the saints
and seek to show hospitality.
ROMANS 12:13 ESV

Depending on your job, you may have hundreds of people
going in and out of the outer circles of your life. You may have
never had a conversation with some of them, but because you
have influenced them in some way, they feel like they have a
connection with you. You don't have to put up a boundary that
gives off a "Do not disturb" aura, but you also shouldn't pretend
that you can be something for them that you will never be.

In certain jobs or ministries, you could encounter many people
whom you counsel, pray, laugh, or cry with. But that's it. They
shouldn't get the bulk of your time, attention, or money. They
don't get to know your heart or influence your decisions. After
a few hours together, you leave those people where they are
and go home to your family and close friends.

*God, there are so many people we can connect with throughout
our week. Help us to be real about what we can be for those
people in our outer circles and to keep our best for those who
are closest to us.*

*Can you find the balance of being welcoming
but not letting everyone in?*

LIMITED RESOURCES

"The LORD is my portion," says my soul,
"Therefore I wait for Him."

LAMENTATIONS 3:24 NASB

Will people ever try to demand more from you than you have decided to offer at their level of intimacy? Sure. This is where you have to honor your boundaries and make sure you do not start treating someone in an outer circle like you treat someone in your inner circles. As soon as you do, you are threatening your relationship with the people who are more important to you because they are the ones who rightfully belong on that level.

Although you can genuinely care about people's needs, you must know that you have limited resources with which to actually meet them, and you should commit those resources to your closest relationships. If you don't, you could be violating the priority of your core connections.

God, please give us the wisdom and grace we need to manage our resources well. We want it to be evident to each other that our relationship is the top priority. Help us take the most care in meeting each other's needs.

How well do you limit your resources?

WITHIN YOUR BOUNDARIES

He's the one who brings peace to your borders,
feeding you the most excellent of fare.
PSALM 147:14 TPT

When you invest consistently in your closest relationships over a period of time, it becomes much easier to honor the boundaries you have set for them. As the value of those relationships increases, other things become less and less capable of competing with that value. You won't feel pressured to take from a close relationship to give to a stranger. You won't struggle with guilt over ignoring a phone call when you are spending time with your spouse.

This is how boundaries work. You say yes to something, which necessarily means saying no to everything else. At first, it may be a challenge to hold on to your yes. The people you say no to make ask for good reasons or struggle to understand, but if you consistently set a firm boundary around your yes, eventually other things won't present themselves as viable options. It becomes a lifestyle to live within your boundaries.

Father, saying no to things (and people!) can be really difficult. We struggle with this at times. Help us to remember the end goal of creating strong connections with our most intimate relationships.

What do you need to say yes to today?

HE SAID NO

There came a man named Jairus,
who was a ruler of the synagogue.
And falling at Jesus' feet,
he implored him to come to his house.

LUKE 8:41 ESV

If you truly want to live the Christian life Jesus modeled, pay attention to the fact that He regularly set boundaries with needy people. Luke 8 records the story of Jesus raising Jairus' daughter from the dead. When the story begins, Jesus has just encountered a whole crowd of people who have been waiting a long time and desperately need something from Him. They know He has the resources and ability to meet their needs, and He has a track record of doing just that.

Somehow, Jairus made it to the front of the crowd and asked Jesus to come heal his little girl. And Jesus made a decision. He said, "Yes." The yes in that moment was also a no to a bunch of other people who all needed healing too. Jesus actually said no to a bunch of desperately needy people? You bet He did. It's right there in the Bible.

Jesus, thank You for showing us that it's most important to pay attention to what the Father wants. Guide us in the way You want us to go. Show us what we should say yes and no to.

How do you feel about Jesus saying no to needy people?

ONE BIG YES

Jesus stopped and said,
"Call him."
MARK 10:49 NIV

We know that Jesus healed all who came to Him on many occasions, but in every case, it was because of His choice. This fact is particularly highlighted in the story of blind Bartimaeus. When he heard Jesus walking past him, Bartimaeus started yelling, "Jesus, Son of David, have mercy on me!" The disciples got irritated and told him to be quiet, but he just got louder. When Jesus asked him what he wanted, Bartimaeus asked for sight, although it seems obvious that would be what he wanted.

Jesus answered with a yes, but it wasn't driven by Bartimaeus' need. Ultimately, Jesus said yes to every person He healed, and no at times to other people, because He had dedicated His life to one big yes: to live out of complete oneness and partnership with His Father. He wanted to be about His Father's business—to do what He was doing and say what He was saying.

Father, You know everything. You see how each little piece of the puzzle of life fits together. You know beyond and outside of our lives. Help us to be about Your business and not our own.

Have you dedicated your life to the one big yes?

AN EMPOWERING YES

"When you have lifted up the Son of Man on the cross, then you will understand that I AM he. I do nothing on my own but say only what the Father taught me. And the one who sent me is with me—he has not deserted me. For I always do what pleases him."

JOHN 8:28-29 NLT

Jesus modeled the big yes that should also define your life. It would likely be impossible to make and keep the boundaries you set around the relationships in your life if you didn't first say yes to your primary relationship with Jesus.

If you don't prioritize your relationship with God, then your God Spot will end up with a human being in it. And that is idolatry.

God, we want to say yes to You first. You give us the perspective we need to take each day as it comes, and to be able to say yes to our most important relationships. Show us where we need to make adjustments in our circles, so we spend our time and energies on the right people.

What does prioritizing your relationship with God look like?

IN THE RIGHT SPOT

The one who loves his brother and sister remains in the Light, and there is nothing in him to cause stumbling.

1 JOHN 2:10 NASB

When you operate as a powerless person, you could allow your spouse or someone else to scoot into the God Spot. This will put your priorities, resources, and relationships out of whack. Your boundaries disappear, and others begin controlling your life. You may feel like your marriage is falling apart. Before you know it, you're trying to escape.

Engaging in an affair or taking up some ridiculous hobby or addiction is unfortunately all too common in these situations. Don't allow it to happen in your relationship. Don't become powerless, afraid, or manipulative, exploiting your relationships in order to survive them. Keep God in the right spot!

God, we humbly come to You and ask You to help us keep our priorities right and our marriage safe. We know how easy it is to wander when things aren't going well. We want to remain powerful in You.

Is it time to reestablish healthy boundaries?

NO COMPETITION

If a person passionately loves God,
he will possess the knowledge of God.
1 CORINTHIANS 8:3 TPT

Putting God first in your life won't compete with your human relationships. It will protect them. One of God's top priorities in His relationship with you is teaching you how to love the people He has put in your life. Keeping God in your God Spot keeps you connected to the Holy Spirit's incredible resources of wisdom and understanding to define your relational priorities and boundaries.

You can rest assured that He will show you who you are supposed to be, whom you should be connecting with, and how to build and protect those connections. He is the Spirit of power, love, and self-control who enables you to follow through on your yes to these relationships.

Holy Spirit, thank You for Your work in our lives. You are always good, always faithful, and always right. Move with power in us as we continue to learn how to love each other, and others, well.

How has the Holy Spirit helped protect your marriage recently?

USING THE TESTS

Be sober, be vigilant, because your adversary the devil walks
about like a roaring lion, seeking whom he may devour.

1 PETER 5:8 NKJV

Will there be challenges to keeping God in your God Spot
and holding on to the big yes? Will there be things that try to
compete with your value for Him, tempt you to violate your
boundaries, and give away to others what only He deserves?
Absolutely. The enemy wants to use these tests to distract you
and ruin your life. But God will use these tests to make you
powerful.

It is powerful when you choose God above all other options,
circumstances, feelings, and desires, especially when the choice
is uncomfortable. Through the Gospel, God has made one
thing abundantly clear: the big yes He asks of you is only what
He has already given you.

*Father, we know the enemy would love to derail us and cause
us to compromise our boundaries. We depend on You for the
strength to choose You and each other every time we are tempted
to do otherwise.*

What tends to compete most with your value for God?

HIGHEST VALUE

Those who are wise will take all this to heart;
they will see in our history the faithful love of the LORD.

PSALM 107:43 NLT

You were each created with a God Spot because God has
given you access to the deepest spot in His heart. He placed
the highest value on His special creation, and His priority is
nothing less than giving you all that He is.

Saying yes to God means saying yes to experiencing the
incredible reality of His love for you. The more you experience
it, the easier it gets to live within the boundaries that keep Him
as the priority in your life and protect the priorities He defines
for your relationships.

*Father, thank You for creating us to love and be loved. Your love
is incomprehensible, unchanging, and just so good. We want
to love like You love and continue to move closer to You and to
each other.*

When did you last experience the reality of God's love for you?

Highway House

So be on guard; then you will not be carried away by the errors
of these wicked people and lose your own secure footing.

2 PETER 3:17 NLT

Boundaries are about the levels of intimacy that are naturally
built into relationships. It is each individual's job to identify
and manage them. Say your life is like a house in front of a
highway, and you have a certain type of relationship with every
vehicle that drives by. One day someone decides to pull into
your driveway and knock on your front door. You answer the
door, and they ask to come in. All of this surprises you, but for
whatever reason, you let them in. They open your refrigerator
and take what they want, and you get a little upset. Then they
go into your bedroom, and you're left wondering what on earth
is happening.

You have to be able to set boundaries as soon as you see the
need for them. Close the door on things that want to get in but
shouldn't. Kick people out of your living room, kitchen, and
bedroom when they have no right being there. Protect your
most important relationships.

*God, we need wisdom in knowing who to allow into our house.
Help us to make and keep boundaries that benefit our marriage
relationship.*

*Are there people you've allowed in your house
that maybe shouldn't be there?*

NATURAL FILTER

Some friendships don't last for long,
but there is one loving friend who is joined to your heart
closer than any other!

PROVERBS 18:24 TPT

You will have noticed differing levels of intimacy and natural barriers in your relationships. In the move from less intimate to more, more is required from you. In the analogy of the house on the highway, lots of people can drive by, but very few people should make it into your bedroom. There is a natural filtering system to relationships, but for whatever reason we don't always pay attention to it.

There could be people in your life who violate levels of intimacy, moving closer without questioning whether they meet the requirements of what it takes to be that close. The more intimacy you have with someone, the more access they have to your core, time, and resources. They get closer to the vital parts of your life, and you communicate what you are thinking and feeling. Save these close levels of intimacy for people who deserve them.

God, You have created us so carefully and perfectly. Thank You for the relational filtering system You have put in place for us. Help us to pay attention to who we are letting get close and to rightly evaluate their influence.

Who do you let in your bedroom?

ROOM FOR ONE

Love each other deeply
with all your heart.
1 PETER 1:22 NLT

Your core, the most intimate part of your life, has room for
maybe two people: you and Jesus. There's nobody who knows
you as intimately as He does. Regardless of your prayer life, He
knows you; He knows everything. This is the most intimate
relationship you could ever have.

Outside of that is your most intimate human relationship.
Here there is room for one: your spouse. Unfortunately, a lot
of people don't let their spouse in that spot for all kinds of
reasons. The closest person to you is the one you have been
the most vulnerable with. You form soul ties with people who
share the deepest part of you. This can be terrifying, but in the
case of your spouse, it should be comforting. It should fill your
need for deep human connection. You and your spouse have
the potential to be the best thing for each other.

*God, we want our marriage relationship to be what You
intended it to be. Help us to be vulnerable and share the
deepest part of ourselves with each other.*

How can you share more of yourself with your spouse?

SCARY PEOPLE

I shall run the way of Your commandments,
For You will enlarge my heart.
PSALM 119:32 NASB

Your immediate family and very close friends should take priority when it comes to your time and resources. Extended family and friends are people you would do a lot for, and neighbors and coworkers a little less. Maybe you have lots of people in your life—ministry, business, community—that have your phone number or email and are vying for your time, energy, and resources. They must carry the least priority.

Because you are a believer, you have the power of the living God inside of you. You have decided to keep your love on, so no matter what other people do to you, you know you don't have permission from God to ever turn your love off. But you can keep the "scary people" in the outermost circle because that's the closest access to you they can handle properly. Hopefully, you never have to put your spouse in that circle (or vice versa), but if abuse and continued disrespect plague your relationship, you don't have a choice.

God, thank You for the grace to keep loving even when it is difficult.

How can you keep your love on even with people you have had to move to your outermost circle?

TEMPORARY SHIFT

Shouldn't you rather have gone into mourning and have put
out of your fellowship the man who has been doing this?

1 CORINTHIANS 5:2 NIV

Moving close people to further away levels of intimacy doesn't
have to be permanent. If someone close to you decides to
experiment with heroin and their life goes off the rails, or
someone is stealing from you or inviting dangerous people into
your home, what can you do? You move them out to the spot
they can handle, which might even be the same level as a total
stranger. You may change the locks on your house because they
can't handle that level of access right now. It doesn't mean it
will be this way forever.

In your closest relationships, you can communicate that there
will always be a place of intimacy open, but they can't be there
right now because of their decisions. If they decide to repent,
they have access to that intimate spot for the rest of their life.
You can hold it for them. Even if you set limits with a loved
one, they still have that place available to them when they can
handle that level of vulnerability.

*God, show us how to handle the tricky situations that come our
way regarding levels of intimacy. We want to be compassionate
and kind, but we also need to be prudent. We need Your
wisdom.*

Are there people in your life who need to move circles temporarily?

COMMUNICATING VALUE

"Do not fear; you are more valuable
than a great number of sparrows."
MATTHEW 10:31 NASB

Creating and applying boundaries comes with many dynamics. You communicate the value and priority of a relationship by the way you give access to your intimacy levels. For each level of access, you set specific boundaries. You communicate to an individual, and everyone who is watching, that they hold a certain value in your life with boundaries.

If you took your wallet and threw it on the floor in the mall and walked away, you would send a message to everyone that there's nothing of value to you in that wallet because everyone has access to it. But, if you took that same wallet to the bank and put it in a vault, everyone who saw it would wonder what you have in it that holds such value.

God, You showed us how much You valued us by sending Your Son to die in our place. Thank You for placing such worth on us. We want to show the people who are closest to us how much we value them by sharing our most intimate space with them.

How do you communicate value?

VANDALS AND THIEVES

"Do not lay up for yourselves treasures on earth, where moth and rust destroy and where thieves break in and steal."
MATTHEW 6:19 ESV

Boundaries communicate value. If you don't have boundaries or levels of intimacy around something, then you send the message that you have no value for it. If you went downtown and found a building with no windows or doors, what of value would you expect to find there? Likely none. Anyone has access to that building. Thieves and vandals can get in and take or break anything they find; they will treat that building however they want.

The same is true of relationships. When you don't put boundaries around yourself, you attract disrespectful relationships (abusive vandals and thieves) into your life.

God, You place a high priority on our lives and on our relationship. Help us to create healthy boundaries that communicate our high value for ourselves and for each other.

How can you set boundaries that communicate value for your relationship and that keep out vandals and thieves?

ON THE WAY TO YES

As Jesus was on his way,
the crowds almost crushed him.

LUKE 8:42 NIV

You must protect what's important to you. The things you've said yes to matter to you. In order to say yes to your priorities, you must say no to other things. Remember the story in Luke 8. Jesus had been batting 1,000—everyone He prayed for received a miracle. The word was getting out as He traveled from city to city. As He approached one city, a group of people came out to meet Him, desperate for miracles. Jarius made his way to the front of the crowd and pleaded with Jesus, asking Him to come heal his daughter. Jesus said yes to this one man and no to everyone else.

Between Jesus and His yes was a crowd of desperate people who wanted to direct His time, energy, and resources. They wanted to be the priority relationships. But Jesus passed through the crowd, meaning He said no to a lot of people on the way to His yes.

God, You always know what's best in every moment of our lives. Thank You for saying yes so many times. And thank You for when You have said no, showing us that we can also say no when it means rightly aligning our priorities.

What can you say no to on the way to your yes?

PROTECT YOUR YES

"Master, everyone is touching you, trying to get close to you.
The crowds are so thick we can't walk through all these people
without being jostled."

LUKE 8:45 TPT

Even though Jesus said no, you may still find it difficult. Maybe
you are worried about upsetting people. The reality is, if you
don't say no to some things, you can't say yes to the important
things. As Jesus passed through the crowd on His way to heal
Jairus' daughter, people were pulling on Him, begging Him
to say yes to them. Then a woman who had been bleeding for
many years reached out in desperation—breaking the rules of
the culture—and grabbed the hem of Jesus' garment. And she
was healed.

When Jesus asked who had touched him, the disciples must
have thought that was a silly question. Who in that town *hadn't*
touched Him? Because Jesus said no to a group of people
putting demands on Him, He was able to say yes to the blind
faith of that woman. If you want to do well in what God has
gifted you to do, you must set boundaries. You must protect
your yes.

*God, give us wisdom to decide what we need to say no to in
order to protect our yes. Show us when we are supposed to
use our gifts to bless others and when we need to ignore the
demands.*

How are you protecting your yes?

A Good Christian

"To sit at my right or left is not for me to grant. These places belong to those for whom they have been prepared."

MARK 10:40 NIV

A powerful lesson in creating healthy relationships is understanding that it's your job to protect your connection to God, each other, your time, your finances, and your health. It's your job to communicate the levels of intimacy and the priorities in them. Desperate people will put demands on you to get what they need, so if you don't protect your important connections, they won't be strong for long. You each have to manage yourselves.

When someone puts a demand on you, asking you to respond like a "good Christian," you need to stop them in their tracks. Remember that protecting your strongest connections is most important. Don't give in to manipulation. You have every right to say you feel like you are being manipulated and you don't respond well to that. If they can't respect your boundaries, the conversation should be over.

Father, we want to protect our most important connections. Show us how to refuse manipulation and control in an effort to prioritize our relationship with You and with each other.

What do you think it looks like to be a good Christian when you are being manipulated by demands?

THE BIGGER YES

"You are a dangerous trap to me. You are seeing things merely from a human point of view, not from God's."
MATTHEW 16:23 NLT

You or your spouse may fit into the category of having a really sensitive conscience. People pick up on this. This know that if they can make you feel bad, they will be able to get you to do what they want. In order to break the cycle of being manipulated by your sensitivity, consider the yes you have for the day that you will not compromise, and put your effort into protecting that yes.

The yes might be spending time with each other or working on a project that really needs to get done. If you don't have the ability to prioritize your own lives, then anyone can derail you with certain manipulation. Sometimes you have to say no. And other times, it might just be a "not today." You don't always have to cut people off entirely, you just need to protect the bigger yes in the moment.

God, thank You for the sensitivity we have toward others. Help us to understand that loving well doesn't always mean saying an immediate yes. Give us discernment in how to handle demands and requests from others.

What is your biggest yes for today?

OFFERING OR ROBBERY

You must decide each in your heart how much to give.
And don't give reluctantly or in response to pressure.
"For God loves a person who gives cheerfully."
2 CORINTHIANS 9:7 NLT

If you were walking through a town with a bunch of homeless people asking for money, you would have two choices. Either you say no freely, or you will be forced to finally say no when you have nothing left. You might be a naturally generous person. Someone else's situation doesn't make you stingy. You have a lot of opportunities to use your resources to practice generosity, but at some point, you will need to practice saying no or you may start avoiding people and places. The difference between a generous offering and a robbery is that you feel powerful. It all comes back to exercising power, being responsible, and feeling safe.

Father, thank You for Your generosity toward us. Thank You that we can share with others. Help us to recognize when we don't need to give and to rest in that decision without feeling bad about it.

How can you remain generous but still practice saying no?

HEALTHY BALANCE

> He saw the disciples straining at the oars, because the wind was against them. Shortly before dawn he went out to them walking on the lake. He was about to pass them by.
>
> MARK 6:48 NIV

How do you balance laying down your life for your friends with setting healthy boundaries? Jesus gave an example. He sent His friends out on a boat and told them He'd meet them on the other side of the sea. Then He went up on a hill to pray. After a while, He noticed His friends, professional fishermen, straining at the oars because of the wind and rain, and the Bible says He was going to pass them by!

How does that sit with you? Is it difficult to think of Jesus ignoring His struggling friends? It's not that He didn't care; He just wasn't going to do anything except what He saw His Father doing. That was His yes. And that's how He could pass by His struggling friends—He had set His face like flint toward the cross.

God, when we look at the bigger picture, Jesus' response to His friends makes a lot of sense. Help us to understand that we need to say no to things that get in the way of the bigger yes.

What healthy boundaries have you set with your friends?

HANDLING OFFENSE

When the days drew near for him to be taken up, he set his face to go to Jerusalem. And he sent messengers ahead of him, who went and entered a village of the Samaritans, to make preparations for him. But the people did not receive him, because his face was set toward Jerusalem.

LUKE 9:51-53 ESV

On the way to His biggest yes, Jesus had to say no. He was headed to the cross, and He wasn't going to stop to do any ministry. It wasn't time for that. The Samarians were not happy about that. If Jesus wasn't going to minister to them, they weren't going to celebrate Him.

The disciples responded the way so many do when people exercise their boundaries—they got offended. They were so appalled by the disrespectful, ungrateful response that they said they would call down fire. Jesus wasn't impressed with their response. When you have to hold your boundaries and say no, you are saying yes to your priorities. You are responsible for those choices, and that means possibly offending people. When the same happens to you, you can choose not to be offended.

God, being offended seems like second nature these days. We want to make the best choices regardless of what people might think or feel. Help us not to be offended when people have to say no to us.

Do you worry too much about offending people with your no?

BACK IN PLACE

It is to one's honor to avoid strife,
but every fool is quick to quarrel.
PROVERBS 20:3 NIV

If someone from an outer circle of intimacy begins skipping levels without building the trust to get there, you may need to consider how you can put them back in the right place in order to protect your more important relationships.

Sometimes this might require verbal communication; other times it could just be changing the time and energy you give to the relationship. Time away from a relationship can help move the intimacy level back to where it should be. There are times when a conversation may be necessary, and that should be navigated carefully but honestly. What you must remember is that closeness with your most important human relationship (your spouse) is your goal.

Father, we want to focus our energies on our relationship. Show us the relationships that we need to move away from and give us the wisdom to know how best to do that.

*Can you think of any relationships that
need to be moved out a level or two?*

PUSH A BUTTON

My child, never drift off course
from these two goals for your life:
to walk in wisdom and to discover your purpose.
Don't ever forget how they empower you.
PROVERBS 3:21 TPT

How many times have you wished you could push a button and someone else would handle all the upset, hurt, scared, needy people who try to pressure, intimidate, and manipulate you? It would certainly make your life easier—at least in theory.

In reality though, it would be better for all concerned if you chose to be powerful and set limits in your relationships. Don't sit and wait for your problems to go away, and don't let other people roll over you. You can take the bull by the horns and create the necessary change.

God, we admit that sometimes it seems like it would be easier to push a button and make the source of all of our conflict go away. But Jesus showed us how to face issues head on, calling out problematic behaviors and challenging us to love with honesty.

Have you been hoping your relational problems will just go away on their own?

REQUIRE RESPECT

You have encircled me with strength for battle;
You have forced those who rose up against me
to bow down under me.

PSALM 18:39 NASB

If you haven't already, you and your spouse need to learn how
to require respect in your relationships. No one wins when
either of you choose to be powerless against your problems.
That will only create more problems. Relationships are
destroyed when you refuse to take responsibility to confront
issues and set limits.

The world is filled with genuinely scary things and people
who are hazardous to your health. Your longtime mortal
enemies—the world, the flesh, and the devil—continue to wage
their campaign to destroy your connection with God and one
another. You won't get through life without encountering threats
and attacks. Learn how to demand respect in your interactions
so your most important relationships remain intact.

*God, we know we need to respect each other, and while that
is hard at times, sometimes it's even more difficult to require
respect from others. Give us the strength to be powerful in
our interactions.*

What does it look like to require respect in your relationships?

EXHILARATING JOURNEY

"The LORD, He is the One who goes before you.
He will be with you, He will not leave you nor forsake you;
do not fear nor be dismayed."

DEUTERONOMY 31:8 NKJV

Nothing less than your eternal destiny is at stake as you learn to fight for your connection, manage your levels of intimacy, and set healthy boundaries around your lives and relationships!

Give up the powerless search for people who can do the dirty work for you and start going after the exhilarating journey of learning to set your own limits and confront your own problems.

God, even when it is uncomfortable to enter into conflict, we know it is necessary to create a stronger connection with each other. Help us to fight together and encourage each other in our efforts to manage intimacy levels and set healthy boundaries.

How can you fight for better connection this week?

LOVE MESSAGES

You make known to me the path of life;
you will fill me with joy in your presence,
with eternal pleasures at your right hand.
PSALM 16:11 NIV

Your lives are a gift from God. They have infinite value to Him, and He communicates this in the many ways He loves you. God is always sending you love messages. If you feel that He does not love you, the odds are you have stopped opening your mail.

If you are struggling to feel God's presence, think about your level of offense. If you have been hurt recently, you might need to clean up your forgiveness. It is most likely the key factor in why you are not feeling love. God doesn't change. He is always full of love for you. Bitterness, offense, and unforgiveness affect your connection with Him. Once you deal with those feelings, get ready to feel the presence of God's love in a fresh way.

God, we see the harm that bitterness does to our connection with You and with each other and we don't want a part of it. Help us to walk in forgiveness so we can sense Your great love again.

Are you harboring bitterness or offense that is affecting your relationship? How can you choose forgiveness today?

GARDEN TO TEND

The LORD God placed the man in the Garden of Eden
to tend and watch over it.

GENESIS 2:15 NLT

After God created the world, He planted a garden and put
Adam in it to tend and keep it. This is a picture of your life.
God has given you a garden to tend. He plants trees in it and
sends the sun and rain to make them grow, but you have the
responsibility to care for the trees and the right to enjoy their
fruit. No one else has that responsibility.

Only by being diligent in managing what is yours will you reap
a harvest that will nourish you and give you something good to
offer others.

*God, there is so much we can tend to in this garden of life. Thank
You for beginning the work, and for helping us maintain all that
You have given us. Help us to continue to nurture the important
aspects of our lives so we can reap the harvest that is coming.*

What parts of your lives need tending right now?

FIRST THINGS FIRST

Now for this very reason also, applying all diligence, in your
faith supply moral excellence, and in your moral excellence,
knowledge, and in your knowledge, self-control, and in your
self-control, perseverance, and in your perseverance, godliness,
and in your godliness, brotherly kindness, and in your
brotherly kindness, love.

2 PETER 1:5-8 NASB

You and your spouse will grow the healthiest relationship when
you each embrace your individual responsibility to tend your
own gardens. You will, of course, both come to the relationship
with needs and participate in meeting one another's needs, but
it is a simple economic principle that you each must be healthy
and fruitful in order to continue offering resources to one
another to meet each other's needs.

The bottom line is that you each need to be able to take care
of yourselves before you can take care of each other or anyone
else for that matter.

*Father, thank You for showing us the need to take care of
ourselves so we are healthy enough to take care of others.
We don't want to become selfish or complacent in our efforts
to care for each other, so help us to discern where that line is.*

What can you do to take care of yourself this week?

YOU FIRST

Delight yourself in the LORD,
and he will give you the desires of your heart.
PSALM 37:4 ESV

If you have ever been on a plane, you have been subjected to the airline spiel about what to do if the cabin loses pressure. They explain that oxygen masks will fall from the ceiling, and they show you how to put them on. Then they remind you that if you are traveling with someone who needs assistance, you should put your mask on before helping anyone else.

The implication is clear. If you don't take care of yourself, then you won't be able to care for anyone else because you'll be lying unconscious in the aisle. The lesson of the oxygen mask exposes the flawed thinking many people have about what it means to serve and love others. Taking care of yourself is not the same as being selfish.

God, we see the need for individual responsibility in order to create a healthier connection. Help us to keep tabs on ourselves and be aware of things we need to take care of so we can offer better help to each other.

What can you do to take care of yourself this week?

SHARED FRUIT

Don't always seek what is best for you
at the expense of another.

1 CORINTHIANS 10:24 TPT

You can cultivate your garden and then choose to keep all your fruit to yourself. You might wrongly use boundaries to be independent and withhold your life from others instead of using them to protect your ability to sustain fruitfulness, generosity, and the exchange of life in your covenant relationships. This is not taking care of yourself; it's just selfish.

Self-protection is not a good motivation for caring for yourself. It will create problems in your relationship when you choose not to be vulnerable or share. Sharing the fruit of your life deepens intimacy.

Father, help us to know the difference between taking care of ourselves and selfishness. We want to share the fruit of our labors with each other and with others.

What fruit can you share together this week?

MAKING IT FLOURISH

Turn my heart toward your statues
and not toward selfish gain.
PSALM 119:36 NIV

You will create many problems if you don't tend your garden. You have to get food from somewhere, and if it's not yours, it will be someone else's. Not taking care of yourself puts you in the powerless position of trying to get other people to meet your needs without being able to offer anything in return. This is a setup for an unhealthy, selfish relationship.

Being loving and unselfish means you will take the time and effort needed to get your garden producing the best fruit possible so you can offer something valuable to others. You will invest in learning all there is to know about making the garden God has given you flourish—from your physical, emotional, mental, and spiritual health to your talents, gifts, callings, finances, relationships, and more. You will protect and sustain your garden's productivity, so your health and the health of your relationships are not threatened.

God, we want to give our best to You first and then to each other. Help us to be productive in producing good fruit, so we can share it with others.

How can you be loving and unselfish this week?

CULTIVATE THE GARDEN

The LORD will guide you continually,
And satisfy your soul in drought,
And strengthen your bones;
You shall be like a watered garden,
And like a spring of water, whose waters do not fail.

ISAIAH 58:11 NKJV

The more you respect the value of your own life by cultivating your garden, the more you will create an atmosphere of respect around you. When people see how you care for your garden and taste the good fruit of your life, their words and behaviors should demonstrate that they recognize your value.

If others don't recognize the value of your life and what you have to offer, you cannot be in relationship with them. The only people you want to connect yourself with are those who respect the value of your life and theirs. When you and your spouse value your own lives and each other's, your relationship will be based on mutual respect and shared fruitfulness.

God, You are the best caretaker of life. Show us how to cultivate our gardens in a way that demonstrates respect for life. Help us to apply value to our own lives and to our relationship.

What does cultivating your garden look like to you?

GARDEN CONSUMERS

Encourage the believers to be passionately devoted to beautiful
works of righteousness by meeting the urgent needs of others
and not be unfruitful.

TITUS 3:14 TPT

The people you need to be able to set boundaries with are the
people who recognize the value of your life but want to relate
to you as consumers. They are attracted to you and the good
things you have to offer, but they are not offering much from
their garden to you.

There are many different types of consumers you will run into.
Some are good, polite people who ask for things nicely. Others
are attractive, and you want to impress them so badly you may
be tempted to offer yourself up for their consumption. Still
others are aggressive, selfish consumers who use intimidation
and manipulation to bleed you. A good relationship with
healthy boundaries is made up of people whose gardens are
equally tended and shared. You need a plan for dealing with all
kinds of consumers who come into your garden.

*God, give us wisdom to set and keep boundaries around our
gardens that don't allow for selfish consumers to come in and
plunder or destroy. Help us to tend to each other's gardens with
honor and respect.*

*How can you assess the types of consumers
you interact with frequently?*

SEAGULLS

Carefully determine what pleases the Lord. Take no part in the
worthless deeds of evil and darkness; instead, expose them.
EPHESIANS 5:10-11 NLT

Seagull consumers are challenging to deal with because they
take one little peck at a time. You may find it easy to let people
like this close to you, giving them the benefit of the doubt as
they peck at your resources. What starts as a few minutes or
dollars may end up surprising you when calculated over a
period of time. If you have a bunch of seagulls pecking at little
pieces of your life, before you know it, your garden will look
like a pumpkin patch in November.

Setting boundaries for seagulls can be difficult because
individually they may only be doing minimal damage. To
preserve the health of your garden, you absolutely must set
limits for how many people you will allow to get near enough
to take pecks, and how many pecks you will let them take.

*Father, it's easy to think that offering ourselves to others is
what we are supposed to do as good Christians. Help us to see
the importance of protecting boundaries, so we have the right
amount to give to the right people at the right time.*

How many seagulls are pecking at your garden right now?

TYPE OF BOUNDARY

We ask God to give you complete knowledge of his will
and to give you spiritual wisdom and understanding.

COLOSSIANS 1:9 NLT

There is a learning process involved in identifying the types
of consumers who want a piece of your life and the kind of
boundaries you need to set with them. There's a difference
between setting boundaries for deer and bunnies. Whether it's
chain-link fences or chicken wire, the purpose of a boundary is
to protect the value of what's inside the garden and keep selfish
consumers out.

The beautiful thing is that when you have the necessary
boundary in place, you don't need to treat consumers like
enemies. If your garden has a fence, you can choose to throw
the produce over for deer or bunnies. With healthy boundaries,
you stay in control of the resources of your life and manage
them toward your priorities.

*God, we see the necessity of setting healthy boundaries. We want
to have the necessary resources first for You, and then for each
other. Guide us in our resource spending; help it to rightly reflect
our priorities.*

What types of boundaries do you need to create?

EXPLOITATION

This is my prayer: that your love may abound more and more in knowledge and depth of insight.

PHILIPPIANS 1:9 NIV

If you cannot set boundaries with consumers, you are going to be exploited. Being misused is not fun. You and your spouse have likely had different experiences where you have been taken advantage of by consumers. What really matters is how you choose to respond to those experiences.

To respond in a way that is powerful, you need to be able to forgive the offense and then figure out how to protect and share your resources more effectively. If you want to build a better connection, you won't let yourselves be disrespected. You'll lose the victim mentality and stop letting people devalue your lives. This will keep you from being fully exploited as individuals and as a couple.

God, we need Your discernment. It can be hard to protect and share our resources effectively. Sometimes we are pulled in different directions. Help us to carefully consider where we are putting our efforts.

Can you see where you have been exploited by consumers?

PECKED CLEAN

Let my passion for life be restored,
tasting joy in every breakthrough you bring to me.
Hold me close to you with a willing spirit
that obeys whatever you say.
PSALM 51:12 TPT

Full exploitation occurs when you allow yourselves to become offended, bitter, and resentful toward those who have taken too much from your resources. You may be wounded or traumatized by past experiences. The seagulls have pecked you to the bone, and it hurts. Maybe someone has been very needy for a long time, and you feel absolutely sucked dry.

You cannot be the only person pouring into a relationship. That will never work. You must recognize where boundaries are not healthy and then set them more appropriately. Instead of blaming others for your problems and becoming bitter, take responsibility for setting poor boundaries and then change them. You can avoid being taken advantage of!

Jesus, even though You gave up everything, it wasn't exploitation because You chose it! You had healthy boundaries in place, and You used Your resources wisely to do the Father's will. Teach us how to be like You in this way.

*Are there people you need to forgive for exploitation?
Do that now and choose to move forward.*

PUSHING BRUISES

He heals the brokenhearted
And binds up their wounds.
PSALM 147:3 NASB

When you are bitter toward someone, every encounter with that person bumps the place of wounding and offense, agitating your pain. They may do the very same thing others are doing to you, but it feels like battery acid being thrown in your eyes when it comes from them. Eventually, you will explode in anger. Blowing up at someone, telling them how horrible they are, and yelling, "Here's a boundary: stay away from me!" is not a good way to set limits.

If you choose bitterness, you will still be wounded. You may find that you have destroyed relationships, and you have no guarantee that you will not be exploited again. This vicious cycle will continue until you become so bitter you turn your love off completely.

Father, we need Your complete healing. Help us to walk in forgiveness and to continue to choose love over bitterness.

Can you identify places of wounding and offense in your life that need healing?

SETTING LIMITS

"May those who love you be secure.
May there be peace within your walls
and security within your citadels."

PSALM 122:6-7 NIV

At times you may have found yourselves in a situation where a coworker, family member, spouse, or best friend decides to start acting like a consumer. These people get to demand more from you because of the access you have given them; they are in the inner circles of intimacy.

If they start pulling on your connection to meet their needs and you don't ever pull back by setting a boundary or asking for them to meet your needs in return, then you are going to be dragging on the ground pretty quickly. The fruitfulness of your garden can diminish at an alarming rate if you do not know how to set boundaries with your close relationships.

Thank You, Holy Spirit, for Your continued guidance and grace over our lives. We trust You to highlight areas where we are allowing our resources to be depleted.

Is it time to set some new limits?

OFFENSIVE BOUNDARIES

Peter took him aside and began to reprimand him for saying such things. "Heaven forbid, Lord," he said. "This will never happen to you!"

MATTHEW 16:22 NLT

Jesus set boundaries with His best friends. Some of the boundaries may have seemed offensive at the time and may seem so to us even as we read the accounts of them now! One time, Jesus was explaining to His disciples that He was going to suffer trial, condemnation, and the cross, and then He would be raised from the dead. Peter didn't want that to happen, and he made it pretty clear. Jesus spun around on His heel and said, "Get behind Me, Satan!"

Jesus called Peter *Satan!* Why? Because, in that moment, He was talking to Satan—the one who ultimately opposed His destiny. Jesus had to set Peter straight. He told Peter he wasn't seeing things through a God lens. Jesus had to set a limit with Peter because he was threatening Jesus' first priority to do His Father's will.

Father, we can find so many things to be offended about. When we try to look at situations through Your eyes, it's easier to walk in grace and make choices that reflect the right priorities. This is what we want for our relationship.

Do you find certain boundaries offensive?
How can you change your perspective on them?

DANGER ZONE

Then Jesus told his disciples, "If anyone would come after me,
let him deny himself and take up his cross and follow me."
MATTHEW 16:24 ESV

Peter was not intentionally trying to get Jesus to disobey God,
but the story illustrates a danger you must both face. The closer
a relationship is to your God Spot, the greater the chance that
the relationship could compete with Him as your top priority. It
all depends on whether you decide to listen to the fear of man.

If the needs and wishes of others—even your spouse—start
to gain a greater hold on your heart's affections and begin
to define your priorities and choices, then you betray your
allegiance to God. This means you align yourself with Satan
like Peter did by elevating the things of men above the things
of God. The Father's priorities alone must define your life and
choices.

*God, what are Your priorities for our lives? We want to align
ourselves with You and walk in a way that demonstrates hearts
that are fully Yours.*

*Are you lining up on the right side,
or are you headed for the danger zone?*

RESPECT THE LINE

For the sake of my family and friends,
I will say, "Peace be within you."
For the sake of the house of the LORD our God,
I will seek your prosperity.

PSALM 122:8-9 NIV

Just like you need to be careful about reserving your God Spot for Him alone, you should also be cautious about demanding or allowing others to put you in their God Spot. Be aware of your propensity to define others' priorities and boundaries. You can encourage, invite, support, and enjoy others as they take responsibility to cultivate their gardens and value the life God has given them, but you must never take over that responsibility.

Respecting the line between your life and the lives of others communicates love. You are essentially telling them that they get to be a whole person in your relationship. And you know how important that is by now.

Father, we want to encourage each other to take responsibility for our own priorities without crossing over lines and becoming too involved. Show us where that balance is.

Is there anyone you find yourself defining priorities for? How can you encourage them without taking responsibility?

CODEPENDENCY

Aspire to lead a calm and peaceful life as you mind your own business and earn your living, just as we've taught you.

1 THESSALONIANS 4:11 TPT

Even if intentions are good, it is not loving to take responsibility for other people's lives. You must be able to see those controlling actions for the destructive force they are. Essentially, you are consuming another person's life and preventing them from becoming powerful, responsible, whole people in the relationship. This is codependency, and it is not healthy.

If you are in any type of relationship with someone who has drug or alcohol problems, it can be easy to fall into this trap. Refusing to confront and hold an addict accountable, and living in a state of denial as to why things are happening a certain way, enables that person to continue living a destructive life. Codependency is driven by the agreement that you will work harder on someone else's problem and life than they do. That is not love.

Father, in Your unlimited mercy and love, You hold us accountable to right living and personal responsibility. Help us not to fall into codependency with anyone. We want to lead people into the freedom from destruction that is only found in You.

Why is codependency unhealthy?

STANDARD OF RESPECT

Let this hope burst forth within you,
releasing a continual joy.
Don't give up in a time of trouble,
but commune with God at all times.

ROMANS 12:12 TPT

It can be one of the most difficult things in the world to set a boundary with someone in your inner circle who is breaking your heart with their choices. But if you want to protect your relationship with that person, you must be powerful enough to hold up your commitment to pursue the standard of respect in your interactions. If the person is consuming too much of your garden for you to stay healthy, you need to limit the access that person has in your life while still keeping your love on.

You are responsible for setting up boundaries, so others do not consume your time, energy, and resources beyond a healthy level. Of course, you can still love them, but you have to protect yourself, your loved ones, and ultimately your relationship with them, by setting limits.

Father, when our hearts are breaking over choices our loved ones are making, help us set boundaries that will guide them back to You. Protect us from the anger and frustration that come with continued poor choices and give us a firm resolve in our demand for respect.

*How do you pursue a standard of respect
in your interactions with people?*

BOLD STATEMENTS

When a man makes a vow to the LORD or takes an oath to obligate himself by a pledge, he must not break his word but must do everything he said.

NUMBERS 30:2 NIV

The best defense is a good offense. You are not going to be successful at setting boundaries if most of your time is spent defending yourself against the requests and demands of consumers. A good plan is making sure your focus is fixed on cultivating the resources of your garden and directing the bulk of your resources toward mutually beneficial, healthy relationships.

In order to carry out this offensive strategy, you need to get really good at telling yourself and others what you are going to do. "I'm going to spend time with the Lord right now." "I've committed that evening to my spouse." "I am taking my mother to an appointment that afternoon." "On Saturdays, I read and study." These statements set boundaries and tell people where you are distributing your resources; they communicate your priorities.

God, give us the boldness we need to state what we are going to spend our time and resources on. Help us to unashamedly commit ourselves to the people and things that are most important in our lives right now.

What does it look like to be less defensive and more offensive in your strategy to set boundaries?

POWERFUL CHOICES

Commit your actions to the LORD,
and your plans will succeed.
PROVERBS 16:3 NLT

As a powerful person, you want to be focused on what you have the power to control—yourself. You also want your choices to be defined by the priorities you have committed yourself to, not by the choices of other people.

When you tell someone what you are going to do, ask yourself if you are making that choice to protect your priorities. Are you only telling them what you will do and not what they need to do? Will you honestly be okay no matter what they decide to do? It's important to be able to answer all of these questions affirmatively. This is how you maintain a successful offense in keeping your boundaries: make powerful choices to communicate them.

Father, we know we only have the power to control ourselves. Remind us of this each time we try to step into the position of controlling each other. Help us to maintain healthy boundaries defined by the priorities we are committed to.

What choices are you making to protect your priorities?

CAPABLE OF NO

Was I vacillating when I wanted to do this?
Do I make my plans according to the flesh,
ready to say "Yes, yes" and "No, no" at the same time?

2 CORINTHIANS 1:17 ESV

In order to be consistent in telling yourself, and others, what you are going to do, you need to be able to complete two other steps. First, you have to be able to follow through on what you say you will do. And second, you need to be able to say what you will not do. Every yes needs to be backed up with action and a clear no to everything else.

Remember, Jesus was able to say no when He needed to: He passed by many people on His way to healing one. And when He saw the disciples in the boat desperately fighting the wind, He had the choice of passing them by too. But He was able to say yes because He was also capable of saying no.

God, sometimes we spend so much time going back and forth on our decisions to follow through. Help us to be people of our word, who do what we say we are going to do and say no to things that take away from our yes.

What can you say yes and no to this week?

WEIGHT OF WORDS

As surely as God is faithful,
our word to you has not been Yes and No.
2 CORINTHIANS 1:18 ESV

When you start telling people what you're going to do and
what you're not going to do, and you follow through on both,
they start to believe what you say. Your words have weight.

The first time either of you turn around and walk out of a
disrespectful conversation, you will probably surprise and
maybe even offend the other person. But this will also set
a standard for being in a healthy relationship and building
connection. If you both want to remain in the room for your
next conversation, you will each manage yourselves and honor
the standard you have set for respectful communication in
your relationship.

*God, it is so easy to say one thing and do another. We let fear
get the best of us too often. Help us give weight to our words and
commit to honoring the standard of respect in our relationship.*

*Have you set a standard for communication
in your relationship?*

LEAVE THE ROOM

Stop being angry!
Turn from your rage!
Do not lose your temper—
it only leads to harm.
PSALM 37:8 NLT

One—or better, both—of you can decide you will no longer contribute to disrespectful conversations. The next time you have a disagreement that leads to no good, stop the conversation. Communicate that you will be happy to finish the conversation when it becomes respectful. Only stay if the conversation remains respectful. If you have to, walk out of the room. Remain calm and self-controlled. You can do this if you have a genuine desire to resolve the conflict.

If you consistently behave the same way in your various disagreements, you will eventually convince each other that you are not going to participate in disrespectful conversations. You will begin to see that you can both control yourselves. You'll adjust your tone and choice of words so you can both remain in the room while you work through your conflict. Try it!

God, we need You to help us remain calm and self-controlled. When we get angry, remind us of the better way.

Have you committed to not being involved in disrespectful conversations?

SET A STANDARD

Love each other with genuine affection,
and take delight in honoring each other.

ROMANS 12:10 NLT

As a couple, you can set a respect standard for conversation whenever you have a conflict. It will become a standard you both prefer because good communication and healthy boundaries give you what you need to stay powerful and maintain your connection. You will find you have more trust, honor, and love for one another, and your conflicts will be resolved in a way where each of you feel safe. This can only happen if you are both willing to change.

The more others encounter you honoring the boundaries you have set for your lives, the more they will know that they can trust you with theirs. Setting and honoring boundaries is essential to creating a relational culture of respect, honor, trust, and love in your connections with people.

God, we desire to treat each other with respect, honoring each other above ourselves. Help us to walk in patience and grace as we develop a healthy standard for discussing difficulties with each other.

Have you established a standard for conversations when conflict is involved?

A MISCONCEPTION

Declare these things; exhort and rebuke with all authority.
Let no one disregard you.

TITUS 2:15 ESV

There is a misconception out there about people with healthy boundaries. Just because you set boundaries, it doesn't mean you don't feel deeply for people. Boundaries are actually one of the best ways to communicate love and value to those around you.

People believe your actions more than they believe your words. The more consistently people encounter the boundaries you've set in your life, the more they can trust that it is you that manages your life. The time, energy, and access you give them communicates true value in your relationships. So, keep your love on and set firm, clear boundaries.

God, help us to embrace this idea that communicating and holding boundaries is loving. It is often seen as harsh, but that isn't where our hearts are. Help us to demonstrate true value and love in our relationship with each other.

How do you view people who create and maintain boundaries?

MOVING ON

"Choose seven men from among you
who are known to be full of the Spirit and wisdom.
We will turn this responsibility over to them."
ACTS 6:3 NIV

It can be difficult to set and communicate limits. You might struggle to identify where the need for the limit is coming from, if your motivation in setting it is right, or what frame of mind you're in when you are communicating it. Separating levels of access with people you care about isn't usually a simple task.

In Acts 6, there is a scene where firm boundaries were set. The apostles had been walking with new converts for some time. The day of Pentecost had been poured out, and there were thousands of people added to the church. One day, the apostles came out and said they wouldn't be waiting on tables anymore; they were going to spend their time praying and studying instead. They passed off their task to other good, capable people, and they moved on. They made it seem easy!

God, show us where we need to separate levels of access with the people we care about. Give us the wisdom to access where things need to be and the boldness to carry out the decisions we come to.

How do you think the church people felt
about the apostles' decision to move on?

STAY STRONG

"That will enable us to give our full attention
to prayer and preaching the word of God."
ACTS 6:4 TPT

It is altogether possible that some of the church people
were upset with the apostles' decision. They didn't like that
their experience was going to be different. Some may have
communicated their feelings. Others might have just left. But it
didn't matter to the apostles because they had communicated
what their priorities were—praying and studying—and they
assigned value to those things by protecting them.

When you set limits with people, don't expect them to be
happy. When you separate who has access to you and who
doesn't, don't expect others to jump for joy, especially if they
get bumped out a circle. People might not believe that you
are canceling on them; they are going to keep coming at
you, testing to see if your no is really no. Stay strong like the
apostles did!

*God, when we know what we are supposed to give our time and
resources to, help us to stick with those commitments. Everything
always works out better when we seek Your wisdom before
making decisions.*

What decision do you need to stand strong in today?

COMMON KNOWLEDGE

As for God, his way is perfect:
The LORD's word is flawless;
he shields all who take refuge in him.
PSALM 18:30 NIV

What do you do when people who have access to your life are not very careful with the responsibility of being close? When people in your life get near you and then become disrespectful or irresponsible, they abuse the place they have with you.

Don't be a victim, and don't look for a rescuer. Be powerful. If someone is violating the spot you've given them, move them out. Set a limit, communicate the limit, and stick to it. Value yourself and your priorities. Move toward a healthy connection with your spouse. Say no to lesser priorities for the sake of each other. Act on your no until it becomes common knowledge that is what you will do.

Father, thank You for Your unconditional love for us. Thank You for Your faithfulness and goodness. Show us how to be powerful in our interactions with those who are mistreating us. Give us courage to hold firm to our convictions.

Are you taking care of your relationship with each other?

THE MIRAGE

Honesty guides good people;
Dishonesty destroys treacherous people.
PROVERBS 11:3 NLT

There might be some people in your life who feel scary. It doesn't work to have other people take care of those people for you. You can't ignore them and hope they will eventually go away. You need to confront people and tell them the truth. You have to test the strength of your connections.

You may have created a mirage type of relationship that appears wonderful; you don't admit to having any conflicts. The reality is, in that situation somebody is violating the relationship and the other isn't telling the truth. This relationship is bound for failure because it isn't real. Honesty is necessary to building a stronger connection.

God, we don't want to avoid confrontation in our relationship. We want to honor each other through it because we know it will happen. Help us to be honest with each other and with those around us.

Does your relationship look like a mirage?

THE SAME BOUNDARY

"I Myself will gather the remnant of My flock out of all the countries where I have driven them, and bring them back to their pasture, and they will be fruitful and multiply."

JEREMIAH 23:3 NASB

Setting boundaries is beneficial to you and your relationship. A boundary keeps in your life what you want to keep in it, and it keeps out what you want to keep out. Imagine letting a toddler out in the yard to play. You better have a fairly good boundary, a fence to keep them in, or else they will just keep going until they find danger. The same boundary that keeps the toddler close is the one that keeps the vicious dog away.

Boundaries in your life can help you retain your joy, peace, love, time, and money. At the same time, boundaries keep out of your life what you want to keep out: disrespect, irresponsibility, and time-consuming, high-maintenance relationships.

Father, thank You for Your Word that shows us clear and healthy boundaries for life. Help us to stay within Your boundaries so we remain under Your protection and care.

What boundaries have you established that keep the good in and the bad out?

MAINTAIN CONTROL

"Your heart will always pursue
what you esteem as your treasure."
MATTHEW 6:21 TPT

Beside keeping the good in and the bad out, boundaries also communicate your priorities. Where you spend your time, energy, and resources determine what value you place on people and things. Your boundaries help you keep control of your time, resources, and energy, and give you the ability to rightly prioritize your relationships.

There are some skills you must develop in order to set and maintain boundaries. It might mean thinking about things a little differently than you have. If you or your spouse have a tough time setting boundaries, you may need to learn how to require respect for things that are important to you. This is easier for some people than it is for others.

Jesus, You were so clear about what was most important to You. You walked in boldness, unashamed of Your boundaries and certain of Your priorities. Help us to be more like You.

Do you find it difficult to require respect from people?

TRUCK MENTALITY

You, O LORD, are a shield about me,
my glory, and the lifter of my head.
PSALM 3:3 ESV

If you or your spouse have a hard time valuing what's in your life, you send a message to those around you that they can come take it. If you can't say no and mean it, because you feel guilty or think it's selfish, people will eventually take advantage of you.

You probably know someone with a truck. Just because they have a truck doesn't mean they should say yes to helping move everyone who asks. Some people are going to see an opportunity for themselves because of their need for a truck, but if the truck owner values their own time, resources, energy, and priorities, they can easily say no whenever a request falls outside of their boundaries. And that is okay. In fact, it's healthy.

God, thank You for all You have blessed us with. We have so much in comparison to many people. Give us the wisdom and strength to say no when we feel our priorities are being jeopardized.

What resources do you think people try to take advantage of in you?

ASSIGN VALUE

The LORD directs the steps of the godly.
He delights in every detail of their lives.
PSALM 37:23 NLT

Demands from the outside will direct you like a video game
if you don't value what is inside your boundary. You need to
learn how to communicate the value you have by saying no
and yes where appropriate. This is speaking the truth in love.
If your yes is somewhat reluctant, you will feel powerless later.
You'll blame other people for the result of that yes.

You have the kind of power that allows you to say no and
yes. Learn to require respect in your life and communicate it
through how you use your yes and your no. Assign value to all
that falls in your boundary, and in doing so, you will rightly
protect it.

Father, thank You for caring about everything we care about.
Show us what we need to keep in our boundaries and how we
need to protect it. Help us speak value to the people who deserve
it in our lives.

What needs value assigned to it today in your lives?

ME NOT YOU

I have set the LORD always before me;
Because He is at my right hand I shall not be moved.
PSALM 16:8 NKJV

It's sometimes easier to tell other people what they have to do than it is to communicate what you are going to do. Remember, you don't control anybody else. On a good day, you control you.

You stay powerful when you tell someone what you will do without telling them what they need to do. If you have a truck, you might tell someone you could help them move on a specific day but not on another. You don't tell them to change the date, fill your truck with gas, be careful with the vehicle, etc. You have no control over any of that—nor should you. Stick with your no or your yes and set the parameters around those answers.

God, we can only control ourselves, and even that is difficult at times. Show us how to communicate without telling people what they need to do. Help us to take ownership of our words.

*Can you communicate what you will do
without saying what someone else needs to do?*

ACTIONS SPEAK LOUDER

Whoever walks in integrity walks securely,
but whoever takes crooked paths will be found out.
PROVERBS 10:9 NIV

Actions speak louder than words. You've probably heard
that many times in your life. It's not your words that people
believe—it's your actions. You might mean to say yes, or even
want to say yes, but that doesn't matter. People will believe your
yes when you do it.

The first time you say you will do something, your spouse
may not believe you. If you follow through and do it, the next
time you say it, they will remember you did what you said
you would. Their response to you will be different. Practice,
behavior, and actions change relationships. Your tears, your
words, and your begging will do nothing. It's your actions
that matter. When you set boundaries, be prepared to take
action, to back up what you say, and to communicate with your
behavior.

*God, thank You that You are a God who stands by Your
promises. You don't utter one careless or empty word. You
always come through for us. Show us how to be more like
You so we can better depend on each other.*

What actions need to take the place of your words?

BUILDING TRUST

Every married man should be gracious to his wife just as he is gracious to himself. And every wife should be tenderly devoted to her husband.

EPHESIANS 5:33 TPT

It may take a while for your spouse to really trust you. Depending on each person's background in relationships, one or both of you may be wary of intentions or expectations. If you continue to move toward each other in your relationship, asking what each other needs, and then working to meet those needs, you will build trust and strengthen your connection.

Your goal should be to remove disconnection and fear wherever you find it. Respond with love to the brokenness you encounter and invite each other to become healthy, powerful, and free. You will both feel loved. Trust, honor, respect, and cooperation will begin to flourish in your relationship.

Trustworthy God, You are the only one who never fails. You meet all of our needs and exceed our expectations at every turn. Show us how to build trust with each other so we can continue to build closeness.

How can you intentionally build trust with each other this week?

THE GOSPEL

While we were still helpless,
at the right time
Christ died for the ungodly.
ROMANS 5:6 NASB

You must get deeply in touch with what the Gospel actually means regarding how you are to relate to God and others. Jesus invited people into a connection with Him, not a religious reform program. He showed up in the midst of your brokenness with compassion and healing. He shocked everyone by how fearless He was about keeping His love on with sinners.

Jesus didn't create distance with broken people; He created connection. But this shouldn't surprise you; His entire mission was to finally remove sin—the source of all relational disconnection—through the cross. This includes your sin, and your spouse's.

Thank You, Jesus, for Your sacrifice on the cross. Thank You for removing our sin and washing us clean. We are broken and in need of Your healing. Teach us to keep our love on for each other even in the messy moments.

What does the Gospel mean to you?

PROPITIATION

My little children, I am writing these things to you so that you may not sin. But if anyone does sin, we have an advocate with the Father, Jesus Christ the righteous. He is the propitiation for our sins, and not for ours only but also for the sins of the whole world.

1 JOHN 2:1-2 ESV

Jesus solved your sin problem for good in that moment on the cross. *Propitiation* is the completely satisfying sacrifice that closes the gap between God and His children. Only Jesus Christ could serve as this sacrifice, and He did. He solved the problem of sin. He solved it for everyone, for all time.

Whether you've sinned once, twice, or a thousand times today, it doesn't change the fact that sin has been taken care of. Whether people admit it or not makes no difference to the fact: Jesus took care of all sin in one moment. Because of that, you have access to the Father.

Father, thank You that we can come to You because Jesus took care of our sin. We ask forgiveness for walking in our own strength, for doing our own thing, for going our own way. We want to align ourselves with You and Your calling for our relationship. Show us what we need to do.

Do you know deep down that your sin has been taken care of?

ACCEPTED

It was necessary for him to be made in every respect like us, his brothers and sisters, so that he could be our merciful and faithful High Priest before God. Then he could offer a sacrifice that would take away the sins of the people.

HEBREWS 2:17 NLT

Don't fall into the mindset that you can only be forgiven and saved at the beginning of your relationship with God. You are washed by the blood of Christ, and you are clean every time you ask for forgiveness.

The acceptance of God isn't conditional. You are wholly and fully accepted—no matter what mess you make, trouble you walk into, or temptation that hounds you. God knows, and He loves you. He doesn't tolerate sin; He lovingly accepts you and shows you the way out.

God, thank You for Your total acceptance of us. We are humbled by Your mercy and grace. Give us the same compassion for each other. When we ask for forgiveness from each other, help us to grant it fully.

How can you adopt God's practice of acceptance in your life?

ILLUSIONS

Being found in appearance as a man, He humbled Himself by becoming obedient to the point of death: death on a cross.

PHILIPPIANS 2:8 NASB

In relationships, it is unfortunately too easy to punish the people you love when they make a mess. You resort to turning your love off and disconnecting the minute sin is exposed. You have no grace for mistakes and expect perfect behavior from everyone in your circles.

The problem with this response to sin is that it is not only completely opposite of how Christ responds to His children, but it also shuts down the possibility of vulnerability and truth in the relationship. Resist the pressure to submit to control by hiding, performing, or agreeing, and choose instead to be honest about your weakness. Genuine humility will lead to a much stronger connection than the illusion of perfection.

Father, thank You for Your grace that covers our sin, and Your strength that is made perfect in our weakness. We want to walk in openness and humility together.

How do you deal with exposed sin in others?

HIDDEN IN DARKNESS

You are all children of the light and children of the day.
We do not belong to the night or to the darkness.

1 THESSALONIANS 5:5 NIV

The problem with responding to sin in a condemning way is that you then have to pretend that you never sin. You have to become excellent at keeping secrets and hiding in the darkness. The deeper you become entangled, the more you have to hide. And the more you hide, the more isolated you become.

You can't be in a healthy, connected relationship if you are unable to admit to your own sin and forgive the sin of your spouse. You are not called to live in the darkness. You are children of the light. There is freedom and healing to be found when you confess to each other and pray together.

Father, show us where we are hiding sin in our hearts. Give us boldness to walk into the light and find freedom from the weight of sin. Help us to encourage each other instead of judging.

Do you tend to hide in the dark or bring your sin into the light?

THE MESS

There is only one Lawgiver,
who is able to save and to destroy.
Who are you to judge another?

JAMES 4:12 NKJV

Being afraid of sin creates false, unattainable expectations based on illusions. If you are afraid of your spouse making mistakes, you won't know how to handle the mess those mistakes inevitably make when they occur—and they will occur. When you have realistic expectations, you know people sin, and you are okay with it because you know "people" includes you.

In a relationship, there will be mess. People aren't perfect, and the sooner you embrace that, the sooner you can move into authentic closeness with your spouse. You can both be vulnerable, knowing your contribution to the mess is probably relatively equal. The best news is that the cross separates you from your mess every time, no matter how big.

Jesus, thank You for Your work on the cross that took our messiness away. Help us to leave our judgments to You and keep our love on with one another.

How do you handle the mess of mistakes in your relationship?

A Brilliant Plan

The Word became human and made his home among us. He
was full of unfailing love and faithfulness. And we have seen
his glory, the glory of the Father's one and only Son.

JOHN 1:14 NLT

Have you ever read the Bible? Believe it or not, it is full of
stories about people who made big messes! But unlike humans,
God never once pretended that the mess-makers weren't going
to blow it. Do you think God was surprised when Adam and
Eve ate the fruit?

God knew exactly what He was getting into when He went into
the people business. He has never been afraid of mess. In fact,
He had the most blindingly brilliant plan for dealing with it
all—the cross. He wants relationship with you even though He
knows you will make messes. And He's right there waiting to
take over the clean-up duty when you ask Him to.

*God, thank You for wanting relationship with us. We are in awe
of Your perfect love that looks at us through the filter of the cross
and sees beyond our sin.*

*How can you embrace the mess
of being in relationship with people?*

LIKE HE LOVES

"This is my commandment:
Love each other in the same way I have loved you."
JOHN 15:12 NLT

By solving the sin problem, Jesus created a safe place—the safest place in the world—for you to be loved, known, accepted, and forgiven. But He gives you one big requirement if you want to live and flourish in that safe place of relationship with Him: you must love one another as He loves you.

If you're not obeying Christ's command to love each other, then you perhaps don't know Him as well as you should. Maybe you don't have much of a relationship with Him at all. As John wrote, "Dear children, let's not merely say that we love each other; let us show the truth by our actions. Our actions will show that we belong to the truth, so we will be confident when we stand before God" (1 John 3:18-19 NLT).

Father, loving like You love is impossible in our own strength. Help us to lean into You and find the love we need to love others well.

What does it look like to love your spouse like Christ loves you?

GIFTED FOR LOVE

If I have the gift of prophecy and know all mysteries and all knowledge, and if I have all faith so as to remove mountains, but do not have love, I am nothing.

1 CORINTHIANS 13:2 NASB

A lot of people think that if they're using their spiritual gifts, they must have a relationship with God. But gifts can be used outside of connection. Gifts can be used without love even. The sign that you are in relationship with Jesus is that you love people—period.

How do you love? Can you open your heart to your spouse and build an intimate connection? Do you understand how to know or be known? Or do you tend to retreat from relationships, thinking that you can be "spiritual" without them? It won't work. Your spiritual calling is nothing less than to love and be loved by God and people. Your spiritual training and growth can only occur in the context of relationship.

Father, thank You for the gifts You have given us. Help us to use our gifts to connect with others, with each other, and with You.

What spiritual gifts can you use to connect with others?

FREE AND UNAFRAID

"If you embrace the truth,
it will release true freedom into your lives."
JOHN 8:32 TPT

The whole nature of relationship is that you cannot control it. All you can control is your free choice to love each other and to receive love. When you make this choice, freedom grows, and fear goes. The sign that you really have love in your relationship is that you and your spouse are free and not afraid.

Free people will tell you the truth. They will make mistakes. This will test the relationship and the state of your heart. It will require you to grow up and become powerful. But the more powerful you become, the more you will be able to hold on to your connection with your spouse and help them as they work through their truth and clean up their mess—just like Jesus does.

God, we want to be free and unafraid. Help us to build connection with each other that allows for vulnerability and honesty. We want to walk in the truth together.

How can you help your spouse today?

HEART TO HEART

> "Then I will declare to them, 'I never knew you;
> depart from Me, you who practice lawlessness!'"
>
> MATTHEW 7:23 NKJV

Have you learned to love? It is the one thing you are responsible for. It is the only thing that God cannot work out for you. No matter what miraculous things God is doing around you and through you, you must never lose sight of this priority. All the signs, wonders, gifts, and supernatural events in the world do not prove that you are connected heart-to-heart with God.

Do you want Jesus to know you? Do you want to know Him? Then love Him and love others. The Bible couldn't be more clear about this: "Whoever loves God, is known by God" (1 Corinthians 8:3 NIV).

God, we want to be known by You. Help us to love others—to love each other—well. Teach us what love really is. We want to be connected to Your heart. Show us what that looks like.

How connected do you feel to God right now?

LEADING IN LOVE

We know that the Son of God has come, and has given us understanding so that we may know Him who is true; and we are in Him who is true, in His Son Jesus Christ. This is the true God and eternal life.

1 JOHN 5:20 NASB

When you really know God, you can do shocking things. You can do powerful things. You can love people whom many would declare unforgiveable and impossible to love. Your lead of forgiveness and reconciliation can cause a ripple effect around you.

You have the ability to choose love. You can create boundaries and still love with your whole heart. You don't need to give fear a place. A full, open heart of love can show you how safe and powerful you truly are.

Father, help us to have compassion for those who seem unlovable. Show us what it means to love fully and without fear. Let us lead others in our demonstration of forgiveness that comes from a heart full of love.

Have you learned to love?

A Bigger Heart

I shall run the way of Your commandments,
For You will enlarge my heart.

PSALM 119:32 NASB

If you are going to keep the one big commandment God gave—to love as He loves—then you need a bigger heart. Secretariat was a freakishly fast champion racehorse who blew contenders away with his shocking, unprecedented stamina. The secret to the horse's incredible power was discovered later—he had a heart nearly three times the size of an average horse's heart.

Imagine what would happen if a bunch of Christians started walking around with hearts three times as powerful and loving as anyone else around them. People might actually start believing that God is real. Ask God for a bigger heart and use it to love those around you well, beginning with your spouse.

Father, we join in the Psalmist's prayer asking for a bigger heart. Give us an undeniable love for others that flows into every facet of our lives and blows people away with kindness, joy, and truth.

Spend some time asking God to enlarge your hearts.

So the World Sees

> "By this all people will know that you are my disciples,
> if you have love for one another."
>
> JOHN 13:35 ESV

It's time for the world to see people who can keep their love on. It's time for the children of God to mature into a company of powerful people who know how to walk in freedom, practice intimacy and vulnerability, clean up their messes, and invite people around them to become powerful, free lovers.

You bear the name of Jesus, and you can become known for carrying His huge heart—the absolutely fearless heart of love that pursues connection with broken sinners. This is how the world will know that you know God. Ask for a big heart and then turn your love on and keep it on no matter what.

Father, thank You for adopting us into Your family and giving us Your name. We want to love without fear and show the world what it means to be part of Your family.

How can you show God's love to the world this week?

POWERFUL DECLARATIONS

The love of God will be perfected within the one who obeys God's Word.

1 JOHN 2:5 TPT

There are some powerful declarations you can speak out and claim over your life that will help you turn your love on and keep it on. Say these together today.

- I know the Spirit of power and love are at work in me.
- I can love at all times through Christ who strengthens me.
- I am courageous with my love.
- I am powerful to control myself no matter what others choose to believe or do.
- My goal is connection, not distance.

Think about what each of these statements means for you right now.

Thank You, Holy Spirit, for Your power and love that are at work in us. Thank You for giving us the strength to love at all times. Help us to work toward our goal of connection as we continue to move toward each other.

Which of these statements was the most difficult to declare? Why do you think that is?

SAY IT BELIEVE IT

The light of God's love shined within us when he sent his matchless Son into the world so that we might live through him.

1 JOHN 4:9 TPT

You can keep your love on and chase fear out of your most vital relationships when you conduct yourselves in these ways and with these thoughts in mind. Say them aloud together now.

- I will tell others about me and let them tell me about them.
- I matter and so do you.
- I clearly and honestly express what I am feeling and what I need to feel.
- I listen well to what others are feeling and what they need to feel.
- I communicate my value and priorities by expecting respect.
- I show respect by listening well and honoring the boundaries of others.

Think about each of these statements and what they might look like practically.

God, thank You for the ability to keep our love on and chase fear away. Help us to walk out these steps in our relationship with each other and with others.

Which of the statements above comes most naturally to you? Why?

DIFFERENT STANDARDS

Differing weights and differing measures—
the LORD detests them both.

PROVERBS 20:10 NIV

Do you judge yourself by your intentions and others by their behavior? Loving unconditionally is learning to love as God loves. How is it that He loves unconditionally, but sometimes it feels impossible to see past someone else's smallest flaw?

You must confront the common thought that says other people's sin is too messy to handle. You are in charge of your willingness to love, and you can choose love every moment of every day.

Father, thank You for giving us the choice to love. You don't demand it and You don't control us; You just love us. You are so patient and merciful with us, letting us choose our own selfish ways and bearing the consequences of turning our love off. We are free to choose and that, in itself, shows us how much You love us. Help us to choose well today, God. We love You.

What can you do to show unconditional love this week?

CHOOSING CRAZY

He has given us this command:
Anyone who loves God
must also love their brother and sister.

1 JOHN 4:21 NIV

Have you learned to love? Do you feel confident before God that you reflect the love of God to the people you come in contact with? It's not always easy to love; sometimes it even feels flat-out wrong to love because the person you are dealing with is so irresponsible and out of control.

The power of keeping your love on can turn lives around. It can change people. You have your limits and you set your boundaries, but you choose when to embrace a crazy situation where you will show love like the Father has for you. And you keep that love on.

God, we pray that the love we have for those out-of-control people in our lives would begin to seep into their hearts. Let them see You through us and come to You to be forever changed by Your love.

Have you learned to love?

LOVE BIGGER

He does not treat us as our sins deserve
or repay us according to our iniquities.
For as high as the heavens are above the earth,
so great is his love for those who fear him.

PSALM 103:10-11 NIV

Keeping your love on means you are willing to sacrifice for someone else's benefit. This is the heart of the Father and what Jesus put on display during His time on the earth. His heart has been planted in you. It's accessible to you so you can move toward the people in your life who need to feel God's love in a tangible way.

The world around you is crying out for love from somebody. Everyone wants to believe that lasting, unconditional love exists. The way they experience it is by running into people like you who have learned to love bigger than anybody they've met.

God, our love pales in comparison to Yours. Your heart is so big we cannot even fathom the tiniest part of it. Help us to love the people around us in big ways. We want to tap into Your love so we can share it with others.

Who do you want to love bigger this week?

REFLECTION OF LOVE

Jesus said to him, "Have I been with you for son long a time, and yet you have not come to know me, Philip? The one who has seen Me has seen the Father; how can you say, 'Show us the Father'?"

JOHN 14:9 NASB

Loving each other like God loves you begins with seeing each other from His perspective. If you knew how precious each of you were to the Father, perhaps that love would begin to flood your being. You were both created to love and to be loved.

You were made to reflect the Father. The disciples asked Jesus to show them the Father, and He was shocked that they didn't already understand. He was so like God in His ability to love that He could confidently say, "If you've seen Me, you've seen Him." You can carry this same heart of love everywhere you go.

God, it is our desire to show Your love to everyone we meet just by extending the love You have given us to them. Help us to see people through Your eyes and with Your heart.

Does your love for each other reflect the Father's love?

THE BATTLE

> Whoever makes a practice of sinning is of the devil, for the devil has been sinning from the beginning. The reason the Son of God appeared was to destroy the works of the devil.
>
> 1 JOHN 3:8 ESV

The enemy's greatest trick is convincing the world he doesn't exist. He would love to deceive you into thinking that other people are the enemy, not him. Just as he did in the Garden, he also continues to plant the deception that you know better— than God or anyone else. If he can get you thinking you're right and your spouse is wrong, and that makes you enemies, he can get you to destroy each other, essentially doing his work for him.

The climate of fear, conflict, chaos, hate, and division in the world today makes it clear that Satan's deceptions are alive and well. Technology amplifies the problem by catering to selfish biases, empowering people to create isolated echo chambers where they reinforce their own views, fears, and suspicions, and become ever more resistant to outside perspectives. You must see this battle for what it is. You and your spouse are on the same side—fight against the enemy together!

God, help us to be more aware of the battle raging around us. We want to fight together to stay together and love each other well.

How can you fight the enemy together?

UNMASKING FEAR

"Blessed is the one who trusts in the LORD,
whose confidence is in him.
They will be like a tree planted by the water
that sends out its roots by the stream.
It does not fear when heat comes;
its leaves are always green.
It has no worries in a year of drought
and never fails to bear fruit."

JEREMIAH 17:7-8 NIV

The antidote to the enemy's deception is recognizing that isolation and mistrust are the most spiritually dangerous places to live. You must open your lives and hearts and learn to build trust with each other.

Trust is formed through the exchange of truth. It grows as you create a safe place where you can both share your thoughts, feelings, and needs. You have to be able to talk about how you are experiencing each other and be willing to adjust in order to build and protect connection. This takes time, risk, and effort, but it is the work of love that brings unity and drives out fear.

Father, we don't want to live in isolation and mistrust. We know You want us to be honest in our relationship with each other. Help us to form trust through exchanging truth with each other. We are committed to working on unity.

What does it look like to unmask fear in your relationship?

GOAL OF CONNECTION

Do not be anxious about anything, but in every situation, by prayer and petition, with thanksgiving, present your requests to God. And the peace of God, which transcends all understanding, will guard your hearts and minds in Christ Jesus.

PHILIPPIANS 4:6-7 NIV

It is critical that you have a clear goal in your conversations—the goal of connection. Embracing the goal of connection means saying, "No matter what our disagreement, I will always elevate the value of you and our relationship above it. At the end of this conversation we may still disagree, but my goal is that we will also still be connected."

When you have the goal of connection, you show up to a conversation with a very specific set of communication tools. Two of the biggest tools that help lower anxiety and close distance during a disagreement are empathy and listening to understand.

God, we want to be connected to You and to each other. Help us to move toward each other with that goal, valuing our relationship above disagreement and conflict. Help us to listen and love well.

How can you develop the tools of lowering anxiety in your communication?

RESPONSIBILITY OF RESPECT

Love must be sincere.
Hate what is evil; cling to what is good.
Be devoted to one another in love.
Honor one another above yourselves.

ROMANS 12:9-10 NIV

Responsibility lies at the core of the culture of honor. Responsibility is literally the ability to respond instead of react. It means going into every situation, conversation, and relationship in your life with a plan for what you are going to do no matter what anyone else does.

Disrespect and disagreement are going to happen in human relationships. If you don't have a plan for how to respond when you encounter them, you only set yourself up to be shocked and reactionary—which is a setup to be the worst version of yourself. In this cultural moment, it has become clear that a lot of people do not have an effective plan for responding to disrespect and disagreement with honor.

God, we want to develop a culture of honor in our home. Help us to respond to situations instead of reacting to them. We want to be the best versions of ourselves in critical moments. Give us Your patience and strength to respond to each other in healthy ways.

What's the difference between responding and reacting?

SPIRITUAL AWARENESS

Throw off your old sinful nature and your former way of life, which is corrupted by lust and deception. Instead, let the Spirit renew your thoughts and attitudes. Put on your new nature, created to be like God—truly righteous and holy.

EPHESIANS 4:22-24 NLT

There are two critical areas of awareness that you will need to grow in if you want to be responsible with your honor. Without this awareness, you will show up to conversations without the ability to see what's really going on behind the surface. The first is spiritual awareness.

At the deepest level of your life, there is a spiritual battle between the voice of love (Holy Spirit) and the voice of fear (the enemy). The voice of fear tricks you into lowering each other's value. The voice of love reminds you that the person you're dealing with is a valuable human being worthy of respect.

God, You created us all in Your image. You love us, and You care for every detail of our lives. Help us to value each other by showing respect and honor. Give us Your eyes to see as You do.

Which voice do you find easier to listen to in moments of difficulty?

EMOTIONAL AWARENESS

Discard every form of dishonesty and lying so that you will be known as one who always speaks the truth, for we all belong to one another. But don't let the passion of your emotions lead you to sin! Don't let anger control you or be fuel for revenge, not for even a day.

EPHESIANS 4:25-26 TPT

The second critical area of awareness is emotional awareness. You need this to determine what lies beneath the surface of your conversation and remain in a culture of honor.

Especially around anger, which is often a secondary emotion, you need emotional awareness. When people feel scared or powerless, anger can be the false power they turn to. When you see anger in your spouse through this lens of emotional awareness, you don't have to react to it. Instead, you can engage with them and try to find out where their fear and powerlessness are coming from. You can work together to reduce fear and lessen anxiety, building closeness and working toward peace.

Father, thank You for creating us as emotional beings. It can be difficult to see through those emotions especially when we feel like we may be the source of them. Show us how to respond to each other with grace and understanding.

How emotionally aware do you think you are?

PANDEMIC

I listen carefully to what God the LORD is saying,
for he speaks peace to his faithful people.
But let them not return to their foolish ways.

PSALM 85:8 NLT

One of the biggest things the COVID-19 pandemic exposed
was the lack of tools many people had to hold effective,
respectful conversations when it really mattered—when people
were scared and hurting.

Most people experienced some level of discomfort during the
first year of the pandemic. At the core of every individual is
the desire for someone to listen to their pain and help them
meet their needs. Everyone wants to feel powerful in powerless
situations, but above that, people want connection. So often,
fear and pain blind them to those deeper needs and cause them
to react in ways that only drive connection away, ensuring their
needs won't be met.

*Father, You are the God of the universe. You knew about the
pandemic long before it ever happened. You know our fears and
our needs without us having to share them. Thank You that You
are our comfort and strength. Help us to support each other in
the times we feel hurt and afraid.*

How were you affected by the pandemic?

CHAOTIC TIDE

The effect of righteousness will be peace,
and the result of righteousness, quietness and trust forever.
ISAIAH 32:17 ESV

Many turned to social media to cope, connect, and stay informed during the pandemic, only to be swept away in a chaotic tide of dishonoring, disrespectful exchanges full of righteous indignation, accusation, and division. Instead of lowering anxiety, gasoline was poured on it. Many lives and relationships are reeling from the pain caused by these interactions.

The most pressing need now in society, and in individual relationships, is to recover and grow in the ability to practice a culture of honor. You and your spouse can become a place of healing and restoration, a place where voices are heard, and differing opinions are respected. A place where chaos becomes peace.

God, forgive us for being quick to speak and slow to listen. Help us to stem the tide of dishonor and disrespect that is so prevalent today. Show us what it means to love well in spite of differing opinions.

Do you sense the need for a shift to the culture of honor in your home?

HONOR, NOT HARMONY

Look at those who are honest and good
for a wonderful future awaits those who love peace.
PSALM 37:37 NLT

A culture of honor is not a culture of harmony and complete
agreement. Such a culture does not exist among humans,
no matter how hard they have tried to create it. In fact, the
number-one driver of dishonor is the belief that if you disagree
with someone, you have permission to devalue, disrespect, and
punish them.

A culture of honor creates the context for powerful people to
show up to a respectful conversation and pursue connection,
listen well, and meet one another's needs regardless of
agreement. It puts the responsibility on each of you not to
demand honor from each other, but to bring your honor to
give away.

*Jesus, You didn't agree with everyone You came into contact with
when You walked on the earth, yet You still showed how much
You valued each one as You sacrificed Your very life for them.
We want to honor each other even when we disagree.*

How can you honor your spouse today?

RECOVERED VALUABLES

"It was fitting to celebrate and be glad,
for this your brother was dead, and is alive;
he was lost, and is found."

LUKE 15:32 ESV

In Luke 15, Jesus tells three parables about lost things: a lost sheep, a lost coin, and a lost son. In each story, the loss isn't a total loss. The shepherd still has ninety-nine sheep safe and sound. The woman still has nine coins accounted for. And the father has another son still at home. Yet the shepherd, woman, and father cannot rest until that which was lost is recovered. When it is, they throw a huge party with their friends to celebrate!

In these parables, the pursuit of the thing that is lost reveals its high value. The passionate search and celebration tell us how precious the sheep, coin, and son were to those who were looking for them. When you truly value each other, you will communicate that value by passionately pursuing your connection.

Father, when we run away from You, You come looking for us as if we are the only people You care about. Thank You for communicating our value through Your endless pursuit of us.

How can you passionately pursue your connection this week?

RELATIONAL LEGACY

Lord, so many times I fail; I fall into disgrace.
But when I trust in you, I have a strong and glorious presence
protecting and anointing me. Forever you're all I need.
PSALM 73:26 TPT

When you got married, you were both handed a box of relational tools, but you have to determine whether those tools are useful or useless. They could be really handy or totally broken. You may come from a long line of broken marriages and families. Somewhere along the line, most of the tools required to build a strong, loving connection that would last a lifetime may have been destroyed or forgotten.

It is possible for you to have better—to not repeat the old cycles of anxiety, self-protection, irresponsibility, powerlessness, unresolved conflict, or disconnection. You can choose to keep your promises to love and protect one another until death and live in a covenant of love and safety.

God, in our relationship, we want our best selves to show up and be seen and known. Help us to leave a wonderful relational legacy for our children and grandchildren.

What kind of relational legacy are you building?

GOOD TOOLS

You need to persevere so that when you have done the will
of God, you will receive what he has promised.
HEBREWS 10:36 NIV

Searching for good relational tools can be a long quest. Finding
what you need to transform your thinking, behavior, and
the culture and quality of connection in your marriage is not
going to be easy. It will take an attitude that determines to
never quit. There will be moments of pain, frustration, and
discouragement which will tempt you to throw in the towel.

Quitting will only ever be a final surrender to the broken past
you are trying to escape. Don't give in. You can find a way out
of the old cycles and strongholds. You can make it through.
You have an incredible Helper who will fight with you and for
you. Use His strength when you can't find your own.

*Holy Spirit, we need You to help us to continue the fight. We
want to give up the broken tools we have been trying to use and
find effective tools that build our relationship. Give us wisdom
to know the difference between those tools.*

What tools have you found to be effective for building connection?

REFUSING TO QUIT

As for you, brethren,
do not grow weary in doing good.
2 THESSALONIANS 3:13 NKJV

Refusing to quit on your relationship isn't going to be something you can do in your own strength. Asking God for help is necessary. Listening to the people He sends to help you is also needed. When you commit to keeping your love on, you will do much better if you surround yourself with people who won't let you quit: friends and family who call you higher. Sometimes others hold the hope you need and the belief that your dream of a healthy marriage can come true.

Continue to seek God together and allow Him to confront and deal with the gaps in your relational toolbox. He can heal you from the past and equip you to do things you may never have seen modeled or thought possible.

Father, help us build emotional awareness and honesty in our relationship. We want to confront our issues bravely and respectfully with repentance and forgiveness, while also exchanging healthy feedback in a language that communicates our love for each other.

How can you champion each other's dreams?

A Delicious Harvest

Don't allow yourselves to be weary in planting good seeds,
for the season of reaping the wonderful harvest you've planted
is coming!

GALATIANS 6:9 TPT

When you and your spouse begin to live with a healthy
relational toolbox—and have the skills to use the tools
effectively—you may understand what that shepherd, woman,
and father felt when the precious thing they'd lost came back
to them. Joy and gratitude will define you, and you will have a
value and appreciation for your connection because you know
what it's like to be lacking that.

Your field full of thorns and toxic plants has been uprooted.
The ground has been fertilized and replanted. And after all
that work, you can finally begin to enjoy a delicious harvest.
Feast on the fruit of your healthy connection—joy, peace, love,
safety, and hope. They taste good.

*God, thank You for Your work in our lives. We are so grateful
that You do not give up on us and that You provide us with the
tools we need to work on creating a healthy connection.*

What fruit are you enjoying in your relationship today?

BEYOND YOU

After you have suffered a little while, the God of all grace,
who has called you to his eternal glory in Christ, will himself
restore, confirm, strengthen, and establish you.

1 PETER 5:10 ESV

When God restores what is lost in your life, and you begin
to live in that restoration, you can't keep it to yourself. That
toolbox, those skills, and the garden you grew with them aren't
just for you. You now have the privilege of partnering with
God to restore what is lost in the lives of others.

This is the message that should burn in your hearts. Look
around the world and see that what was lost in your lives is lost
in so many others. Many people today are children of divorce.
Family and relational breakdown has affected everyone to
some degree. No matter your history of broken tools and
broken relationships, you can build a new future and leave a
better legacy for your spouse, children, grandchildren, friends,
coworkers, and communities.

*Thank You, God, that You are a god of restoration. You bring
wholeness where there is brokenness and pain. Help us to reach
out to those around us who need to see You at work in their
relationships.*

Who can you reach out to and encourage this week?

ASK, SEEK, KNOCK

"Keep on asking, and you will receive what you ask for.
Keep on seeking, and you will find.
Keep on knocking, and the door will be opened to you."

MATTHEW 7:7 NLT

God is the great restorer, the filler of the gaps. He can pick up the pieces and bring healing that causes transformation in you, so you can help bring healing to others. If you've been on the quest to recover what's been lost in your life and feel weary waiting for breakthrough, don't give up! Keep asking, seeking, and knocking. The Father is not holding out on you—He is seeking your restoration passionately, despite what you see, and He will bring it about.

God's heart for those affected by the breakdown of families and relationships is that they would become family and relationship restorers. When you know what it feels like to lose something, and you fight to get it back, you become people who celebrate the value of connection. You treasure it, and you urge others to do the same.

Father, thank You for pursuing our restoration. You have given us strength when we were weak, and grace to move toward each other even in our pain. Show us how we can be part of a generation of relationship restorers.

What breakthrough have you seen in your relationships?

LOVE TRANSFER

Now let me speak to the wives. Be devoted to your own husbands, so that even if some of them do not obey the Word of God, your kind conduct may win them over without you saying a thing.

1 PETER 3:1 TPT

As two powerful people, you and your spouse can build an incredible connection. A vital key in your relationship is understanding that the foundation of it is the idea of connecting. You cannot transfer "I love you very much" back and forth without connecting.

When you lose your internet, your life seems to stop. This is similar to when you have a disconnect in your relationship. It starts with you, and it moves out from there. You cannot make your spouse love you. In a healthy relationship, you understand that there's a choice involved. There is a responsibility that you both have when it comes to building your vital connection with each other.

God, help us to remain connected to You and to each other. We know this is an important part of growing together and keeping our love on. Thank You for always being near.

How connected do you feel to each other right now?

FOUNDATION FOR LOVE

We are His workmanship,
created in Christ Jesus for good works,
which God prepared beforehand that we should walk in them.
EPHESIANS 2:10 NKJV

The foundation for love is that you carry a posture everywhere you go that says you choose your spouse. It's not based on what they have done before or on whether they choose you. You tell yourself what to do, and you do it. You have the capacity to manage yourself in your relationships.

When God says, "I choose you," what He communicates is that you won't ever have to worry about His half of the relationship. He will manage that. You take care of your half, but no matter how that goes, He won't change His posture. He will always choose you. Can you do the same in your relationships?

God, it seems impossible to fathom how You choose us every minute of every day when we often fail to do the same. We want to learn this from You, so we can practice it in our relationships with others. Give us the grace to love like You do.

How are you managing your respective halves of your relationship?

MANAGING ME

The grace of God has appeared, bringing salvation to all
people, instructing us to deny ungodliness and worldly desires
and to live sensibly, righteously, and in a godly manner in the
present age.

TITUS 2:11-12 NASB

Powerless people think the world around them is much more
powerful than they are. They constantly look for things to gain
control of and manipulate so they'll be all right. The idea that
others make them _____ (angry, miserable, happy, etc.)
communicates that it is those other people's job to manage
them. But this is not true.

The reality is you control yourself. You make yourself mad,
sad, content, or whatever else. No one else controls you. You
can choose to be powerful and manage yourself. You decide
to keep your love on let everyone else decide how they will
respond.

*Father, what seems so simple is actually more difficult than we
realize. We don't want to fall into the trap of believing that it is
someone else's job to manage us. Help us to take responsibility
for ourselves and to walk in a way that communicates that to
each other.*

*How easy or difficult is it for you
to relinquish your control in this area?*

KEEP THE FLOW

Husbands, you in turn must treat your wives with tenderness, viewing them as feminine partners who deserve to be honored, for they are co-heirs with you of the divine grace of lice, so that nothing will hinder your prayers.

1 PETER 3:7 TPT

The goal for you and your spouse is that you have two powerful people in your relationship. You require that you each bring high levels of respect and responsibility to your relationship. If one of you comes in low in that area, the other one will let them know. You'll say what they are doing isn't working for you, that it feels disrespectful, scary, or hurtful when they behave a certain way. Once you have shared that, you expect that your spouse will manage whatever they need to manage on their side to protect your connection.

Powerful people work together in a culture of honor, building a strong connection that allows "I love you very much" to flow back and forth with ease.

God, give us boldness and patience to share openly with each other in ways that bring better connection to our relationship. We want our love to flow freely back and forth.

Take a moment to evaluate the level of respect and responsibility you are bringing to your relationship.

RESPECTFUL INTERACTION

As those who have been chosen of God, holy and beloved,
put on a heart of compassion, kindness, humility,
gentleness, and patience.

COLOSSIANS 3:12 NASB

You need to be a good listener if you're going to do conflict
effectively. Establish some rules. You can't both talk at the same
time; collective monologue will not provide understanding.
Somebody needs to have the role of seeking to understand. If
you aren't sure who that should be, default to being the listener
yourself, and create a place where acceptance is high, and
anxiety is low.

Successful conflict resolution comes when you are willing
to serve each other, when you're vulnerable and honest, and
when your ultimate goal is connection. Tell your spouse about
what's happening inside of you. Let them see you and be
committed to finding out what they need too. This respectful
interaction is necessary for resolving conflict and protecting
your connection.

*God, forgive us for when we have not sought understanding
and peace. Thank You, Jesus, for showing us how to be selfless
servant leaders with boundaries and no compromise.*

How respectful are your conflict interactions?

GOD'S GIFT

"Even the Son of Man came not to be served but to serve others and to give his life as a ransom for many."

MARK 10:45 NLT

Powerful people take responsibility for their yes. They don't blame other people for not saying no. They don't *end up with* a life; they *build* a life they intend to live in, one that God has called them to and ordained them in.

Jesus left heaven and came to the earth as a helpless babe. He didn't blame God for the decision, or the hardships suffered because of it. He built His life around God's purpose and prioritized things that led to His ultimate yes. He was God's gift to mankind, and He fully embraced that role. He set limits, took responsibility, and managed His side of every relationship regardless of what He got in return. *That* is powerful.

Father God, thank You for sending Your Son as a gift to the world. We are in awe of Your grace and mercy today. Jesus, we want to follow Your example of learning to say yes by learning to say no.

How are you taking responsibility for your yes today?

PROTECTING VITAL PIECES

I want them to be encouraged and knit together by strong ties
of love. I want them to have complete confidence that they
understand God's mysterious plan, which is Christ himself.
COLOSSIANS 2:2 NLT

Your relationship goal is connection. In communication you
should both be committed to lowering anxiety as much as you
can. Manage yourselves and don't try to control each other. You
don't know what your spouse is going to do, and that is okay.
Just focus on what you are going to do. This is how you create
effective boundaries.

Boundaries exist to ensure that you stay powerful where you
are powerful, that you protect what it is that you're going to
protect—the vital pieces of your relationship. Whether it's
respect, responsibility, love, or honor, you have an opportunity
through the conduct of your boundaries to actually see what
you said was important to you come to pass.

*God, we see the importance of setting boundaries to help protect
the vital pieces of our relationship. Help us to create effective
boundaries and to be responsible for sticking with them for the
sake of our connection.*

What are the vital pieces of your relationship?

UNFORGIVENESS MONSTER

Tolerate the weaknesses of those in the family of faith,
forgiving one another in the same way you have been
graciously forgiven by Jesus Christ. If you find fault with
someone, release this same gift of forgiveness to them.

COLOSSIANS 3:13 TPT

A healthy relationship requires both of you to walk in a
spirit of forgiveness. When you refuse to forgive each other,
you often set up a case and tell other people about what has
happened to you, trying to pull them onto your side. This
presents the beginning of dividing your kingdom—your home.

When you hold on to unforgiveness, you also bring division
in the kingdom of heaven. You operate in an opposite spirit,
inviting fear into the situation and into your relationship.
That enemy of love begins warring against what God is trying
to do. You have to see unforgiveness for the monster that it
is. But you can defeat it. Choose to forgive and let go of your
bitterness.

*God, we are sorry for holding onto unforgiveness and allowing
bitterness to settle in our hearts. Please uproot it in us and help
us to burn it all in the fire of Your love and grace.*

Is there any unforgiveness lodged in your heart?

BEHAVIOR OF COVENANT

"If you forgive other people when they sin against you, your heavenly Father will also forgive you. But if you do not forgive others their sins, your Father will not forgive your sins."
MATTHEW 6:14-15 NIV

Forgiveness is a behavior of covenant. Keeping a covenant requires death, and that means being willing to die to your case, to seeking justice the way you would prescribe it. It's not in your power to handle a situation the way God would. Trust your King, your Father, to be the judge in the situation. Seek reconciliation and restoration. When you turn your love on through forgiveness, fear and vengeance are drained from the relationship.

Unforgiveness is not an option. It's toxic. It's dangerous. And it leads to a place of disconnect. Consider your relationship. Make sure it is free of vengeance and anxiety, which are evidence of ongoing disconnect where you've changed your goal from pursuit and connection to feeling satisfied in disconnection.

God, we know that forgiveness from the heart is a condition of a right relationship with You. Show us how to walk in forgiveness and grace each day as we move toward each other in love.

What does the word covenant mean to you?

REMEMBERED FOREVER

Concerning brotherly love you have no need for anyone to write to you, for you yourselves have been taught by God to love one another.

1 THESSALONIANS 4:9 ESV

Love is often super inconvenient and scary. It can hurt. But loving well can also change lives. It can bring people out of dark situations and communicate the intense, pursuing love of Jesus. The people who love well are the people who are remembered forever. They support you, challenge you, and encourage you to never quit—even when your decisions could cost them considerably.

If you play a part in preparing someone for their destiny in God, you should count that an honor and a privilege no matter what it costs you. That is bearing Christlike fruit. And that is what it looks like to keep your love on.

God, we want to be people who love others and each other well. Help us to illuminate the world with Your light and life. Your kindness and mercy are so good we can't help but share them with others. Give us the determination to keep our love on even when it is inconvenient and scary.

How have you seen God's love change lives recently?

ACTIVATING LOVE

This is his commandment:
We must believe in the name of his Son, Jesus Christ,
and love one another, just as he commanded us.

1 JOHN 3:23 NLT

You are called to live from your heart, to carry the love of Jesus everywhere you go, and to be convincing, willing to sacrifice and go farther than you think you can. You can have an incredible amount of love pumping through you when you connect to the heart of God.

Activating God's love in your life will cause you to stand out so far beyond what anybody has experienced of love in their lifetime. It will allow you to take large steps toward each other in your relationship and give you the confidence to manage your boundaries carefully. With your love kept on, you can bolster and protect a healthy relationship together.

God, we need Your never ending, unfailing, radical love in our lives. Help us to connect to Your heart and draw from Your everlasting source of love and goodness. We want to minister to those around us in ways that show supernatural love and grace. Show us how.

How will you seek to activate God's love in your lives?

YES AND AMEN

All the promises of God in Him are Yes, and in Him Amen,
to the glory of God through us.

2 CORINTHIANS 1:20 NKJV

Capture the impartation and gift that you have: you can change outcomes because you leave your love on. You can protect your connection, learn ways to communicate that decrease anxiety, and champion with love against love's enemy—fear. You can set boundaries, learn how to value what's been put in your life, and know how to say yes or no.

It is possible to good care of yourself. Through all of this, you become a champion of love. When people look at you, it will feel like they are experiencing the Father.

Father, thank You for this gift of love You've given us. Enlarge our hearts so we increase our capacity and better understand what it means to love unconditionally. Give us wisdom, strength, and great courage to do life well and finish the race.

Can you answer "yes and amen" to the question of whether or not you have learned to love for His glory?

ABOUT THE AUTHOR

Danny Silk serves on the Senior Leadership Team of both Bethel Church in Redding, CA and Jesus Culture in Sacramento, CA. He is the President and Co-Founder of Loving on Purpose, a ministry to families and communities worldwide. Danny is also the author of six books covering subjects of building successful relationships, a culture of honor, and strong families. Danny and Sheri got married in 1984 and currently live in Shingle Springs, CA. They have three children and three grandchildren.